God, Where are you?

Why do bad things happen? Why do prayers go unanswered?

Stan J. Tharp, D. Min.

2017

Dedicated in loving memory to Ken Venable, a true friend. Little did we imagine as we shared lunch the day Ken challenged me to write this book, that he wouldn't live 7 months longer to get his gift copy from me. He modeled how to trust God, how to live life, and how to love others when bad things happen and prayers don't get answered.

TABLE OF CONTENTS

Introducing: The Problem of Pain...5

Chapter 1: Two days from Hell and five amazing words...11

Chapter 2: The tip of an iceberg..25

Chapter 3: God answers prayer...46

Chapter 4: Really bad spiritual advice................................55

Chapter 5: "Everything happens for a reason"...................70

Chapter 6: Four "causes" for everything............................83

Chapter 7: "Now What?" 13 suggestions..........................101

Note: All Biblical references are from the New American Standard Version of the Bible unless otherwise noted. The Lockman Foundation. Anaheim, California: Foundation Publications. 1995.

INTRODUCTION: The problem of pain: (Why bad things happen and prayers don't get answered).

Life can hurt; life can disappoint. At times, life hurts for all of us. Try as we might to escape it, pain and disappointment are unavoidable. A certain amount pain and disappointment will happen to us all.

Sooner or later, most of us will encounter pain that seems unbearable, disappointment that shatters our dreams, or evil that leaves a dreadful scar on our soul. In addition to the blatant variety of suffering, there are the subtle, lingering hurts and struggles that create a cloud of sadness, regret, or isolation. These pains seem to follow us and diminish what we hoped or dreamed life would be.

The little pains, injustices, and disappointments we typically take in stride. But the big hurts - tragic losses and ongoing, overwhelming sufferings - are the experiences that devastate us.

> *Pain is hard to endure. Pain can be even harder to understand. Pain is often impossible to explain or accept.*

We struggle with questions: Where is God in all of this? How do I make sense of this? Why did it happen? What did I do to deserve this? We wonder if there is any hope to deal with the evil and injustices in our world.

The problem gets even more complicated for those of us who believe or have been taught about an all-powerful, all-loving God. How can such a God allow all the pain in our world, or worse, cause it? I've been in the room filled with raw emotions and aching hearts as a loving family said goodbye to their dying teenage son; a loss that, to this day, doesn't make sense. I've stood at the bedside of a dying friend as brain seizures sporadically caused him to writhe in pain until he lost consciousness. He didn't do anything to deserve such agony. I've struggled for words that felt empty as I sat trying to comfort a mother whose son took his own life. I have found no suitable answers when someone asks why the rape or incestuous incident happened to them.

Horrific physical pain, overwhelming personal losses, and soul-scarring evil deeds are laced throughout this journey we call life. Some seem to experience more than others, but no one seems immune.

More frequent calamities include the pain of a job loss, marital breakup, or the average car accident which causes certain financial and logistical hardships and perhaps a trip to the emergency room for some level of medical care.

Add to this the everyday ouch experiences: a stubbed toe, a car door slammed too soon, a snide remark we aren't sure we were meant to hear, or a social media post spreading hurtful rhetoric across the web. Pain is hard to endure. Pain can be even harder to understand. Pain is often impossible to explain or accept.

Evil is pain intentionally caused by someone else. Whether the evil is a schoolyard bully who taunts a child because they're overweight, or the evil of a sexual bully (predator) who imposes their lustful will onto an innocent victim, the pain of evil inflicted by another adds to the unbearable nature of such suffering.

Somehow, it is easier to cope with our pain if we are able to understand it. The problem is that much pain and suffering doesn't make sense. No amount of reasoning can explain away all evil, injustice, or the painful suffering of the innocent. This is a core struggle for humanity.

Philosophers refer to this as "The Problem of Pain" or "The Problem of Evil." The struggle is a problem in two regards. First, and most obvious, is simply the tangible problem that pain, suffering, and evil present us in our personal lives. We hurt. We struggle. We bear the impact. We want to understand in hopes of avoiding such pain in the future, so we often ask "Why did this happen?" and "How did this happen?"

The second problem caused by evil and pain is for one's worldview. It is difficult to reconcile pain and evil into a worldview that includes an all-powerful God who is also all-good and loving. C.S. Lewis defines the problem of pain (in his book of the same name):

> "If God were good, He would wish to make His creatures perfectly happy, and if God were all-mighty He would be able to do what He wished. But the creatures are not

happy. Therefore God lacks either goodness, or power, or both." [1]

If one presumes there is no God, at least pain and suffering fits their worldview. A worldview that excludes God often involves a cosmology of the universe that is harsh and impersonal where pain is simply a random result of chance.

Still, this stoic acceptance of pain and evil is uncustomary for most humans. Even devout atheists can wince inwardly at the thought of unjust evil or unwarranted pain. Philosophies of pop culture karma are thrown about as we like to think that people get what they deserve, yet so much of the pain and evil in the universe is unmerited and uncalled for.

This book offers no response to the atheist. Their world is one that was begun and is sustained from nothing, for no explainable reason, by chance. The world of the atheist has no reason to be fair or comfortable. Any pain or evil, even the most agonizing and horrendous is neither underserved nor justified, it simply is. Atheists can save themselves the emotional anguish of their struggles by choosing to accept the reality of pain in life without necessarily having to justify or understand it.

This book, however, is for those of us who believe in a creator who has revealed Himself to be all-powerful and perfectly good. This book seeks to wrestle with the pain,

---

[1] C.S.Lewis. The Problem of Pain. Harper One Publishers. New York: 1996. P. 26.

disappointments and evil in life. It doesn't necessarily provide every answer to "Why?" It does offer a perspective that may help us cope with not knowing, while still trusting in an all-powerful and perfectly good God.

CHAPTER INTRODUCTION:

CHAPTER ONE: Two days from Hell and five amazing words.

"And the Lord said to Satan, 'Have you considered my servant Job? For there is no one like him on the Earth, a blameless and upright man, fearing God and turning away from evil.'" Job 1: 8

> Job is perhaps the greatest example in all of history of a "good person." He had such integrity. Job was kindhearted, he was a family man. He was successful and "blessed."

We will consider Job throughout this book because he is a good example of bad things happening to a good person. We see this as we read of two divinely permitted horrific days. Job's identity as a dad vanished overnight when all of his ten children were killed by a natural disaster. Job also suffered the loss of his physical health, his wealth, and his marriage was devastated.

On top of all this, Job had to endure a barrage of self-righteous condemnation from "friends" accusing him of some unknown sin that must have caused his calamity. In their minds, bad things happen to bad people (and vice-versa).

Job must be examined by all who ever wondered "why" in the face of adversity or pain. He as a perfect case study. We can both identify with, and learn from him. Meet Job.

CHAPTER ONE: Two days from Hell and five amazing words.

The Bible offers a biographical study in "Why bad things happen to good people and prayers go unanswered." It is the account of a traumatic season in the life of a man named Job (the "o" is long as in "go," not as in "I need a job").

If there was ever a proverbial "day from Hell," it is recorded in Job 1: 6-9. In fact there is a secondary "day from Hell" in the next chapter, (Job 2: 7-9). These days are delivered like a one-two knockout punch in a cage match to one of the nicest, most undeserving people on the planet.

Scholars believe Job's biography is perhaps the oldest book in the Bible. Since this story is thousands of years old, this problem for Job (and humanity) appears to have existed throughout history. The problem can be condensed this way: If God is all-powerful and all-loving and just, why do bad things happen to good people, and why do their prayers seem to go unanswered? Struggling souls might simply ask "God, where are you?" Let's examine the life of our good, unfortunate friend for some insights.

> *It seems to have started with an amazing day in an incredible life that went horrendously wrong.*

It seems to have started with an amazing day in an incredible life that went horrendously wrong. Job is a "good" man (when the Bible says you're good, that's quite an endorsement!) He is a devout family man according to the customs of his day. Job honors, loves and serves God. Job practices what he preaches and lives out his goodness with his family. Job is also wealthy, very wealthy. Readers will typically fall short of resenting his prosperity because at least he is such a "good guy."

Read this description as recorded in Job 1: 1-5 (The Living Bible).

> *"There was a man in the land of Uz whose name was Job; and that man was blameless, upright, fearing God and turning away from evil. Seven sons and three daughters were born to him. His possessions also were 7,000 sheep, 3,000 camels, 500 yoke of oxen, 500 female donkeys, and very many servants; and that man was the greatest of all the men in the east.*
>
> *His sons used to go and hold a feast in the house of each one on his day, and they would send and invite their three sisters to eat and drink with them.*
>
> *When the days of feasting had completed their cycle, Job would send and consecrate them, rising up early in the morning and offering burnt offerings according to the number of them all; for Job said, "Perhaps my sons have sinned and cursed God in their hearts." This Job did continually.*

When it comes to wealth, Job is the Bill Gates of his day, and the kind of spiritually devout family man who inspires father's day cards. His kids throw spectacular birthday parties, Job would offer religious sacrifices just in case they sinfully misbehaved in their partying. Job is an exceptionally good guy. He's so good, that God brags about him in a curious meeting of beings in the spiritual realm. Read of it in Job 1: 6-8 (The Living Bible).

> *"One day as the angels came to present themselves before the Lord, Satan, the Accuser, came with them. 'Where have you come from?' the Lord asked Satan.*
>
> *And Satan replied, 'from earth, where I've been watching everything that's going on.'*
>
> *Then the Lord asked Satan, 'Have you considered my servant Job? He is the finest man in all the earth-a good man who fears God and will have nothing to do with evil.'"*

Somewhat surprisingly, God accepts Satan's spiritual "dare" and gives permission to put Job to the test.

The point of this encounter appears to be to declare Job's exemplary goodness. He lives what he believes and practices righteousness in his daily life. Additionally, he's been blessed; not only is Job wealthy in material goods. Job also has many children. In ancient times this too was considered an abundant blessing. Job had 7 sons and 3 daughters. Truly, Job is a case where a very good person is experiencing a very good life.

Satan (the accuser) challenges God's view of Job. He questions Job's righteousness. Satan sarcastically scoffs at Job's reputation. Satan claims that Job is a good person because his goodness is so well-rewarded. He claims Job will quit serving God when the good-life stops: *"Just take away his wealth and he'll curse you (God) to your face"* (Job. 1:11 The Living Bible).

Somewhat surprisingly, God accepts Satan's spiritual dare and gives permission to put Job to the test. Satan receives permission to "do anything you like to his wealth," but he is forbidden to do Job personal physical harm. This is perhaps the first "cringe point" for the average God-believing reader. What follows in Job's life is horrible. It is every parent's nightmare, and while God doesn't cause it, He clearly allowed it. This introduces the reader to a discomforting level of personal vulnerability. It raises the daunting question: "If God would allow such tragedy to happen in the life of righteous Job, what would He allow to happen to me?"

> *In one day, Job's whole identity had been totally destroyed. He was no longer successful, no longer wealthy and no longer comfortable. Worse than all these losses, Job was no longer "Dad."*

In the following verses the "Day from Hell" is unleashed. Enemies (The Sabeans) raided and killed his donkeys, oxen and farm staff. An apparent lightning strike (fire from heaven) killed all his sheep and herdsmen. Three other bands of enemies (Chaldeans) drove off Job's camels and killed his servants. More thorough than any stock market crash, in one horrendous day, Job's net worth is wiped out and reduced to zero.

The old adage "When it rains it pours" could easily have been invented this day. The Bible says as the message bearer was telling Job about his camel loss, another servant came with a parent's greatest fear. He told Job while his children were all feasting in the oldest brother's home, something like a tornado destroyed the house and killed all the inhabitants. Job is now both penniless and childless in one tragic day.

The pain of Job's loss was devastating. The loss of his fortune would pale in comparison to the loss of his children, all ten of them! Not only is this a tangible and relational loss to Job; this is also a loss of identity. In one day, Job's whole identity had been totally destroyed. He was no longer successful, no longer wealthy and no longer comfortable. Worse than all these losses, Job was no longer "Dad." Decades of fatherhood were taken from him, leaving him only memories of a lifetime spent raising his little boys and girls into men and women.

The single, most amazing aspect about Job in the midst of his tragedy is his response. Job's response was *appropriate*, *unexpected* and *exemplary*.

Job's response was *appropriate.* He had the customary extreme grief reaction of his day; he tore his robe and shaved his head. This outward display of inner heartache would have begun a customary period of mourning that would last for many days. In this we learn it is ok to grieve our losses and pain.

> *We understand and expect Job's grief reaction, but choosing to worship God in the midst of heart ache captures us by surprise, it is an unexpected, atypical and exemplary response.*

Job's response was also *unexpected.* Job 1:20 tells us he fell to the ground. This is not the unexpected part. We would also expect Job to respond along the lines of "Why me God? Why my children?" On the contrary, Job does what few of us tend to do in the onslaught of heartbreaking tragedy. The Bible says in this horrible moment, *"Job fell to the ground and worshipped"* (Job 1: 20).

Worship literally means "reverent honor paid to God."[2] It is about expressing adoring reverence to God, and ascribing the immeasurable worth due to a perfect, powerful, loving deity. We understand and expect Job's grief reaction, but choosing to worship God in the midst of heartache captures us by surprise. It is an unexpected, atypical, and *exemplary* response.

---

[2] Dictionary.com

Again, Satan meets Job's worshipful response with skepticism and sarcasm at yet another meeting of spiritual beings in God's presence. This time it is after the "Day from Hell." God once again boasts on His servant Job:

> *"There is no one like him on the earth, a blameless and upright man, fearing God and turning away from evil. And he still holds fast his integrity, although you incited me against him to ruin him without cause"* (Job 2:3).

Satan mocks God's interpretation of Job. He claims Job's righteousness will fail, and Job will curse God to His face (2:5) if Satan is given permission to afflict Job in his physical health. To the reader's dismay, Satan is once again given divine permission to afflict Job. The only limitation is Satan must spare Job's life.

As a side note, this is yet another troubling verse for the person of faith. While God doesn't cause it, He now gives permission for satanically inflicted physical disease and suffering in Job's body. This begs the question, "So does God allow physical suffering in my body?"

> *Days into the suffering, the smell and sight of Job's hurting body would be repulsive.*

Our poor, devastated hero is dealt another anguishing blow:

"Satan went out from the presence of the Lord, and smote

Job with sore boils from the sole of his foot to the crown of his head." (Job 2: 7)

What agony! Job was smitten with painfully infected sores all over his body. Lacking any medical attention, Job uses a broken piece of pottery to scrape the tops off the puss-filled sores in order to drain the swelling infection in hopes of getting some relief.

Try to imagine his throbbing, miserable pain. No doubt the constantly swelling, draining sores make rest and sleep nearly impossible. Days into the suffering, the smell and sight of Job's hurting body would be repulsive. The disease drove him from his home; our righteous, godly hero sits amidst the ashes of an extinguished garbage-burning dump. Think about that sad scene.

> *For Job's wife, all hope was gone. God certainly showed no evidence of His existence or care, death seemed better than a continuing miserable life.*

Job's wife had been attacked as well; not physically, but certainly she was reeling from their instant loss of wealth and devastated with grief at the loss of their ten children. Overwhelming, unexpected and undeserved pain often prompts a bitter response. Such was the condition of Job's wife's heart. The pain, dread, and loss of her world left her wounded, hopeless, and angry. She advised her now physically-infirmed husband: *"Do you still hold fast your integrity? Curse God and die!"* (Job 2: 9).

For Job's wife, all hope was gone. God certainly showed no evidence of His existence or concern. Death seemed better than a continuing miserable life. She questioned Job to the core. First, *she challenged his character*. She asked, "Do you still hold fast your integrity?" Throughout this crisis, Job has taken the high road. He did not blame God nor did he fall into depressing self-pity. Job maintained his faith and kept himself from lashing out in anger or despair. Job's wife then went beyond insulting his integrity to *mocking Job's faith*. She added insult to injury.

The last quote heard from Job's wife is her caustic, *"Curse God and die!"* (Job 2: 9). A person can often resist insults to their integrity and mocking of their faith when it comes from outside sources. In some circumstances such outward opposition can actually make a person stronger. However, when the insults and mockery come from those closest to us, people who we trusted (like a spouse), the verbal assault can be as devastating as the painful situation itself. Many of us have made the same discovery that Job made. Those closest to us can wound, burden, and defeat us soul-deep.

The fact that Job lost his fortune, his family and his health in two horrific days sets his life apart as an illustration of heartache. While uncommon, certainly others throughout history have gone through similar loss. What makes Job stand out from the majority of suffering humanity is *his appropriate, unexpected,* and *exemplary* response.

In Job 1: 21 he worships God with the prose of praise:

> *"Naked I came from my mother's womb, and naked I shall return there. The Lord gave and the Lord has taken away. Blessed be the name of the Lord."*

> *For Job to speak no blame or bitterness reveals a tender, righteous heart that is dependent on God.*

Worship is certainly not the typical response of those in anguish. Yet, Job reveals his deep love for and trust in God. His confronting words for his wife in 2:10 reveal his humility. Job is willing to accept whatever might come his way without questioning God: *"Shall we accept good from God and not accept adversity?"*

Job is as accused; he is a man of integrity. His beliefs shape his words and his behavior. The most astounding aspect of Job's response to this tragedy is five amazing words, *"Nor did he blame God"* (Job 1:22). Job refused to blame God for being unfair, unjust, uncaring or unloving or somehow not powerful enough to protect him and his blessed life. Another amazing statement is in this same verse, *"In all this Job did not sin with his lips."*

Job's behavior calls to mind the words of Jesus. Jesus taught that our words reflect the depths of our heart. What a person says, will eventually reveal what they believe:

> *"The good man out of the good treasure of his heart brings forth what is good; and the evil man out of the evil treasure brings forth what is evil; for his mouth speaks from that which fills his heart"* (Luke 6: 45).

For Job to speak no blame or bitterness reveals a tender, righteous heart that is dependent on God. His profession of faith matches his practice, God is worthy of praise and can be trusted. A later chapter will consider Job's theology. Testing helps clarify belief. Some of Job's beliefs are refined through this ordeal, but he begins this journey with a pure heart, unblaming lips, and trust in God.

APPLICATION AND REFLECTION:

Reading Job's tragic story does two things: *First*, it puts most of our suffering and loss into perspective. The old adage, "It could be worse" comes to mind when comparing our problems to his. Still, our sufferings and losses are real. Just because Job's pain was unusually severe, it doesn't serve to minimize our own.

Many of us have our own smaller version of "days from Hell." We know what it is like to lose a loved one. Grief can be immobilizing. Financial loss is common, whether it be through a devastating stock market "adjustment," a failed business venture, or personal bankruptcy. Physical disease and suffering hits us all. Most of the time we recover, and regain our health, however, many times we or our loved ones do not. Marital, family or relational strife and pain also tears at our very souls.

Second, Job's story prompts us to consider the questions that plagued him, and that were debated by his friends. People offer both welcomed and unsolicited advice and comfort just like today. We may lay awake at night wondering "Why? What did I do to deserve this? How did this happen? How did I end up here?"

1. What feelings and questions re-surface when we remember painful life events, sufferings or disappointments?
2. How have others responded to your painful circumstances, in both helpful and unhelpful ways?
3. How have you found yourself responding to God in the midst of your hardship? Have you ever questioned or blamed God? Why?

CHAPTER INTRODUCTION:

CHAPTER TWO: The tip of an iceberg, not the center of the universe.

"Have I sinned? What have I done to you, O watcher of men? Why have you set me as your target, so that I am a burden to myself? Why then do you not pardon my transgressions and take away my iniquity? For now I will lie down in the dust and you will seek me, but I will not be." Job 7: 20, 21

> Suffering, pain, and disappointment tend to narrow our focus and attention onto ourselves and our world. Throughout the book of Job, he questions God repeatedly for the answers and for the reason behind his tragedy. No answers come.
>
> Suffering is the "iceberg tip" of a universe-wide calamity. There is a cosmic war raging between good and evil, between God and Satan. Personalizing and reducing all suffering down to "why me" is about as appropriate as a baseball fan in the stands demanding answers from a batter about why his foul ball struck him. The batter could rightly answer "There's a big-league game going on and you just happened to be negatively impacted by a foul ball. It isn't personal or anything about you."
>
> Likewise, there is a "big-league" conflict raging throughout the universe and pain is a by-product. It helps to consider the nature of the conflict of good and evil before asking "Why me?"

CHAPTER TWO: The tip of an iceberg, not the center of the universe.

For many people, the common question in response to suffering is "why me?" This question places our struggle at the center of the universe as we demand answers from God. "Why did you let this happen? God, why didn't you protect me? Why didn't you answer my prayers? What did I do wrong? Why do I (or we) deserve this?"

> *Death, sickness, suffering and evil were never intended to be something for humans to experience, they are the collateral damage to humanity in Satan's war against God, the by-products of sin.*

The pain and suffering we experience is more like the tip of an iceberg in the universe rather than the center of it. In order to properly consider why bad things happen and prayers go unanswered, we need to "zoom out" from the pain and evil experienced in our personal lives. We need to consider evil in situations broader than that which might happen at a community level. We must even ask our questions in a context grander than the pain and suffering and injustice that occur at national and global levels (like genocide and tsunamis).

To adequately consider the problem of evil and pain we must consider the universe. Since nearly the beginning of time, the problem of evil has been wrapped up in the nature of all creation.

At the most macro-levels of spiritual existence, the universe is at war. Divine good versus horrendous evil, God versus Lucifer, eternal life against sin. Death, sickness, suffering, and evil were never intended to be something for humans to experience; they are the collateral damage to humanity in Satan's war against God, the by-products of sin (Romans 5: 12).

Pain, suffering and evil don't just happen in a moral vacuum. The conflict is due to an inherent duality in the universe: good and bad, right and wrong, just and unjust, righteous and evil. This duality transcends the physical world of what we see and sense. The contrasting natures of the universe are at the core of creation and are nearly timeless. To develop a healthy response to why bad things happen and prayers go unanswered, we must consider the creation account of the universe and try to understand our place in the hostile battle between good and evil.

In the gospel of John (1:1) the Apostle indicates that "God created the universe of spirit beings and matter. Spirit beings are assigned jurisdictional responsibilities in governing the universe. Lucifer (Satan or the Devil) has jurisdiction over Earth. He rebelled against God and became the father of sin (evil), and is at war with God for control of Earth. This animosity toward everything and everyone God has made explains Satan's hateful adversarial role in Job's life. (John 1:1-4, 14: 30; Isaiah 14: 12-14; Ephesians 6:12; Daniel 10: 12,13; Revelation 12: 7-9, 20: 1-10; Ezekiel 28: 11-15; Matthew 4: 8-11)." [3]

Humanity was created to have a relationship with God. In this relationship mankind was given a redemptive, subduing responsibility for the Earth. The Earth had already spiritually fallen due to Lucifer's rebellion before Adam and Eve were even created. (Genesis 1: 26-28; 2 Corinthians 5: 17-19). Eager to destroy what God had created, Lucifer sought to bring humanity down to destruction.

> *This animosity toward all and everyone God has made explains Satan's hateful adversarial role in Job's life.*

Unfortunately, mankind succumbed quickly to Satan's temptation to evil and chose disobedience and self-reliance instead of submission to the divine will of God. Adam and Eve abandoned their divinely appointed mission before they could even pass it along to the next generation.

God was unwilling to abandon Earth and humanity to Satan's agenda of destruction. "Helpless to restore himself, man became the object of God's love in Jesus Christ, who made provision for man to be reconciled to God and regenerated so that man can again walk in fellowship with God and resume his original divine mission in life. This redemption, reconciliation and regeneration provided by Christ's atonement must be personally experienced by each individual who would benefit from it.

---

[3] Richard D. Dobbins. "Benefits of Sanctification." Pastoral Psychology Workshop. Series I, number 8. Emerge Ministries. 1979. P. 1.

Jesus called this being born again (John 3: 3, 15-17; 5: 15-21; 1 Corinthians 3: 5-10; Romans 10: 9-17)."[4]

The universe is spiritually fallen from the originally intended divine order. Sin is evident and has been yielded to in every human life. No one has or can escape this truth (Romans 3: 23). No one is sinless. God could have easily divested Himself of this spiritual struggle. He could have washed His hands of the evil, pain, and sin of the world and allowed Earth and humanity to spiral into oblivion. However, God loved humanity and His creation too much to abandon it to evil and suffering. The life and mission of Jesus Christ is evidence of God's refusal to surrender the universe: *"The Son of Man has come to seek and save that which was lost"* Luke 19: 10.

> *God was unwilling to abandon Earth and humanity to Satan's agenda of destruction.*

Satan was expelled from God's divine heavenly domain and banished to Hell. Hell is a place that was clearly not created for humanity, but as Christ said, "For the Devil and his angels" (Matthew 25a; 41; Revelation 20: 10). Lucifer appears to be filled with an everlasting revengeful rage, seeking to destroy all God has made. He especially seeks to destroy humanity; he wants as many humans as possible to end up in hell with him. Jesus summarized Satan's hideous hateful purpose as *"to steal, kill and destroy"* (John 10: 1).

---

[4] Ibid. p. 1.

As part of this sinister strategy, "Satan shifted the focus of Adam's attention from fellowship with God to the fruit of the forbidden tree, by appealing to man's senses. As such, Adam's priorities were reversed—the fruit of the tree came first, then fellowship with God. Matter was prioritized before spirit. After the fall, man found himself sensually alive to the material world, but spiritually dead to the things of God. Paul refers to this as spiritual blindness in 2 Corinthians 4: 4."[5]

> *God could have "washed His hands" of the evil, pain and sin of the world and allowed Earth and humanity to spiral into oblivion.*

Satan's onslaught and Adam and Eve's tragic complicit responses are known as "the fall of man." In Genesis chapter three the human centerpiece of God's creation was now spiritually and physically damaged and distorted from their original divinely intended role and identity. Paul explains in 1 Corinthians 2: 14 that the human mind lost its original created capacity to respond to "eternal life" (the force that emanates from God).

---

[5] Dobbins. P. 5.

In his spiritually fallen state, "the unregenerate man is insensitive to the presence of God's creative life about him. He is cut off from eternal life because of sin's impairment of his mind and the distortion of his physical longings and aspirations."[6]

> *Lucifer's fall incited his eternal hateful quest against God and all God has created.*

Lucifer's fall incited his eternal hateful quest against God and all God has created. The fall of man was a key strategic victory for Satan in this futile but universe-wide conflict. This conflict is real, continues today, and is the ultimate reason for pain and suffering; it rages between God and Satan through the forces of sin and eternal life.

"Sin is an invisible force emanating from Satan which stimulates the mind of man to consider life options which fulfill Satan's mission to steal, kill and destroy humanity's creative potential" (John 10:10). Eternal life (from the Greek word Zoë) is an invisible force emanating from God which stimulates the mind of man to consider creative, righteous life choices (John 3: 16)."[7]

Humanity is fascinated by the possibilities of sinful choices. We refer to this preoccupation as "temptation." When such thoughts are acted out, they become sin and are an observable expression of us yielding to Satan's tempting efforts in this universe-wide battle between good and evil, between eternal life (Zoë) and eternal death (sin).

---

[6] Dobbins. p. 6
[7] Ibid. p. 7

In contrast to sin, God's mercy and amazing grace are evidenced in eternal life. This is God's gift to a fallen planet through His son Jesus Christ (John 3: 1). In our natural state the Bible says that humans are incapable of understanding or responding to the concept of spiritual realities and eternal life (2 Corinthians 4:4; 1 Corinthians 2: 14). It is the work of the Holy Spirit in the human spirit that makes eternal life possible for humanity (John 3: 3).

Our experiences of personal pain, daily unfairness and injustices and outstanding times of horrific suffering are not just about us. They are the tip of a much larger iceberg. They are personalized manifestations of this grand universe-wide war between good and evil that rages between Satan and God for the redemption or destruction of the universe.

> *Rather than turning to God for comfort, Satan echoes the advice of Job's wife in our souls and hopes we will follow it in the midst of life's heartaches and "curse God and die."*

When "the problem of evil" is seen from this grander perspective, it makes less sense to ask "Why me?" as though the positive or negative events in our personal lives are what ultimately matter. No one is immune from the effects of evil as this cosmic battle rages; no individual is the sole and exclusive recipient of the workings of evil.

We all struggle. All humans know hurt. No one is excluded from Satan's vengeful obsession to steal, kill, and destroy.

Satan's goal is for sinful temptations to spiritually pollute and destroy our God-given potential and to rob us of our divinely intended eternal heavenly destination. If sin can't tempt us to disqualifying disobedience, Satan hopes that as suffering and evil cause pain in our lives, we will relinquish our redeemed identity and heavenly inheritance by blaming our creator for allowing our suffering. Rather than turning to God for comfort, Satan echoes the advice of Job's wife in our souls and hopes we will follow it in the midst of life's heartaches and "curse God and die."

> *Our adversary the Devil would like to utilize this fallen-ness in our own demise.*

Either way, whether we succumb to sin, rage against God in resentment, or simply live in spiritually unaware futility, Satan seeks to eternally distance us from God and seal our own eventual fate with him in Hell. This universal battle between good (God) and evil (Satan) is the true reason for sin, suffering and evil on the planet, and in our lives. The fallen-ness of the planet (and the universe) is inescapable as a common experience of its inhabitants. Our adversary the Devil would like to utilize this fallen-ness in our own demise.

To adequately consider the problem of evil we must also clearly comprehend God's response to sin. Sin is not just our harmless moral mistakes. In his book *Knowing God* J.I.

Packer identifies such a flippant perspective with paganism. Pagans "tend to dismiss a bad conscience, in themselves and others, as an unhealthy psychological freak, a sign of disease and mental aberration rather than an index of moral reality...they imagine God as a magnified image of themselves and assume that God shares His own complacency about Himself. The thought of themselves as creatures fallen from God's sight, fit only for God's condemnation (and judgement) never enters their heads."[8]

People tend to question and blame God in and about their suffering. The idea of Hell or any earthly suffering as judgment from God raises even more human accusations and blame against God. The spiritual reality revealed in the Bible is that wrongdoers, sinners, actually have no hope of anything but God's retributive judgment. Such judgment is a recurring theme throughout the Bible, culminating in the scene of the final and ultimate Great White Throne Judgment recorded in Revelation 20: 11-15.

Throughout history God has often acted in judgment on Earth. Those who angrily question God's judgments misunderstand that one of the primary motivations for God's acts of judgment is mercy, in hopes of drawing the guilty to a place of restorative repentance (2 Chronicles 6: 36-40).

---

[8] J.I. Packer. Knowing God. Downers Grove Illinois: InterVarsity Press. 1973. P. 130.

Hell is God's ultimate judgment. Originally created only for the Devil and his angels, it is the eternal destiny of all who die in their unrepentant evil (sins). Many ignore God's role as a just judge. Under the guise of grace they reject any thoughts of God's wrath as harsh, cruel and inconsistent. "Speak to these people of God as a father, a friend a helper, one who loves us despite all our weaknesses and folly and sin, and their faces light up. But speak to them of God as judge and they recoil from such an idea."[9]

> *People who do not accurately read the Bible confidently assure us that when we move from Old Testament to the New Testament, the theme of divine judgment fades into obscurity.*

However, the Bible is filled with references to God's judgment. (Genesis 3: 6-8; Exodus 7-12; Judges 2-4; 1 Kings 17, 22, 23). Jesus himself is both savior and judge. Acts 10: 42 tells us *"He is the one who has been designated by God as judge of the living and the dead."*

The contemporary mind is comfortable with an enabling image of a loving God who wishes His creatures would be holy, but He settles for far less in us because He totally understands how hard it is! Such casual grace and compromising holiness insults and demeans the character of God. "Unless one knows and feels the truth that

---

[9] Ibid. p. 39.

wrongdoers have no natural hope of anything from God but retributive judgement, one can never share the Biblical faith in divine (amazing) grace."[10]

> *God wants us, His creatures to live an abundant life in the midst of a fallen universe, while becoming a redeemed and contagious representation of His righteousness...*

"People who do not accurately read the Bible confidently assure us that when we move from Old Testament to the New Testament, the theme of divine judgment fades into obscurity. But if we examine the New Testament, even in the most cursory way, we find at once that the Old Testament emphasis on God's action as just judge, far from being reduced, is actually intensified.

The entire New Testament is overshadowed by the certainty of a coming day of universal judgment, and by the problem arising: How may we sinners get right with God while there is yet time?"[11]

God as judge is not inconsistent with His perfect love and moral goodness. On the contrary, as J.I. Packer asked, "...the truth is that part of God's moral perfection is His perfection in judgment. Would a God who did not care about the difference between right and wrong be a good and amiable God?"[12] Would a God who put no distinction

---

[10] Ibid. p. 131.
[11] Ibid. p. 140.

between the Hitlers and the Mother Theresa's of the world be praiseworthy and perfect? Moral indifference would be a blatant flaw, not perfection. Not to judge the world would be a moral failure of God. "The final proof that God is a perfect moral being is the fact that He has committed Himself to judge the world."[13]

So far in this chapter we have identified that God is good, and His goodness actively generates the spiritual force of eternal life (Zoë). When a person responds to the promptings of the Holy Spirit and accepts and yields to eternal life (through accepting Christ as their personal savior) a personal spiritual relationship with God is established.

> *God as judge is not inconsistent with His perfect love and moral goodness.*

Eternal life is a force which enables the believer to live a life of abundance with the help of God's Holy Spirit (John 10: 10, 16: 7-15). Accepting Christ into one's life places us directly on the "good" side of the universal battle between good and evil. Becoming a Christ-follower means we have joined in the spiritual conflict. The Apostle Paul reminds us:

> *"Our struggle is not against flesh and blood, but against the rulers, against the powers, against the world forces of this darkness and against the*

---

[12] Ibid. p. 143.
[13] Ibid. p. 143.

spiritual forces of wickedness in the heavenly places." (Ephesians 6: 12)

However, Satan's pain-spreading, evil-inflicting and destructive agenda is not reserved only for Christians. Every human being, by nature of being part of God's creation is subject to evil and pain. For the non-believing atheist there should be no real "problem of evil." The question "Why bad things happen?" can simply be met with "Why not?" C.S. Lewis reminds us that belief in the loving and powerful previously mentioned God who is the source of eternal life, in some ways "creates, rather than solves, the problem of pain, for pain would be no problem unless, side-by-side with our daily experience of this painful world, we had received what we think a good assurance that ultimate reality (God Himself) is righteous and loving."[14]

A final consideration in realizing our suffering as part of a universe-wide conflict is to understand the nature and importance of free will. Love is of supreme value to God. Love by definition is a choice. Love cannot be forced or demanded. Love is a response that is soul-deep. In His infinite wisdom, God enabled the boundless possibility of love by giving His creation free-will. It was God's intention that spirit (angels) and human beings would exercise their free will to love and serve Him.

That angels and humans would have a love of the divine is an appropriate response to God who loved us first, at the

---

[14] C.S.Lewis. p. 14.

moment of our conception. As the Apostle John reminds us, *"We love because He first loved us." (1 John 4: 10, 19).*

As previously noted, angelic and human free will went bad. Perhaps this even happened in ways that a perfectly loving God couldn't have initially anticipated. Satan chose not to love and submit to God, humanity soon followed suit. This rebellion opened the floodgates of evil and pain into creation. This was the most costly and tragic choice possible, passed along through the entire human race.

It is important to acknowledge a few facts about God that can help us wrestle with pain, evil, free will and better understand why bad things happen to good people:

1. God's love is perfect. He established His creation with the intentions of having a reciprocal, loving relationship with both spirit beings and human beings. And no matter what you do, whether you choose to follow Him or not, God loves you.
2. God places supreme value on free will and rarely chooses to over-ride it (Deuteronomy 30: 19, 20); even when the outcome of free will is painful.
3. As love is at the core of God's identity so also is justice. In fact, if God is to be a God of love and He is all powerful, He must also be a God of justice. Otherwise, His tolerance of hideous evil with no recourse would make Him somewhat of an enabler.
4. If God were only a God of love and justice, every human being would someday face eternity in Hell. All humans are guilty of sin (evil) according to

Romans 3: 23. As such, they are deserving of sjudgement regardless of God's love

5. However, God is also a God of grace and mercy.
God's grace means we can receive God's mercy and favor even though we can do nothing to earn it:

> *God places supreme value on free will and rarely chooses to over-ride it.*

For by grace you have been saved through faith; and that not of yourselves, it is the gift of God; not as a result of works, that no one should boast." (Ephesians 2: 8, 9).

6. God's mercy is part of the greatness of God in that He is willing to bestow His grace rather than the judgment we deserve (Luke 1: 49, 50).

7. God's ultimate Earthly goal for human beings is that they accept the promise of eternal life through Jesus Christ (John 3: 16) and then live a journey where the greatest goal in the context of this relationship is to accomplish God's purposes and be conformed to His righteousness in our personal lives (Matthew 6: 33).

These seven facts add up into quite a different God of the Bible than the God we often hope or act like He is. When we bend these qualities to our liking, to serve our needs, the problems of evil and pain abound.

> *When we "zoom-out" to a universe-wide view of evil and pain... the problem of evil and pain in our daily lives takes on a different meaning.*

C.S. Lewis confronts our self-defined understanding of the goodness of God. "By the goodness of God we mean nowadays almost exclusively His lovingkindness; and in this we may be right. By love; in this context, most of us mean kindness- a desire to see others than the self-happy; not happy in this way or that, but just happy. What would really satisfy us would be a God who said of anything we happened to like doing, 'What does it matter so long as they are contented?' We want, in fact, not so much a father in Heaven as a grandfather in Heaven- a senile benevolence who, as they say, 'liked to see young people enjoying themselves, and whose plan for the universe was simply, that it might be truly said at the end of each day, a good time was had by all.'"[15]

This human-serving, comfort-prioritizing pain-avoiding kind of God is definitely the way we humans would like for God to be. However, a more mature and less self-centered awareness of His nature in the context of our fallen universe makes it clear God is not "all about" our comfort and enjoyment in our earthly lives. God is about His

---

[15] C.C. Lewis. P. 31.

creatures living an abundant life (John 10: 10) in the midst of a fallen universe, while becoming a redeemed and contagious representation of His righteousness, until we are someday restored to our unfallen intended glory in God's presence forever in a new Heaven and a new Earth (Revelation 21: 1) untainted by evil, unfamiliar with even the concept of pain.

When we "zoom-out" to a universe-wide view of evil and pain, and a creation-wide understanding of the nature and desires of God, the problem of evil and pain in our daily lives takes on a different meaning. Pain, evil and injustice will always be a source of anguish and even torment for the human soul in our earthly lives. However, rightly interpreted, our heartache is more over the reality that it exists at all, rather than the struggles of why evil is encountered and injures our personal well-being.

As such, evil and suffering can actually be instrumental for God to accomplish His greater and eternal purposes in shaping the human heart. Pain does not allow us to deny the fallen nature of the universe, or our fallen selves, in the pursuit of temporal yet fleeting happiness. "Pain insists on being attended to, God whispers to us in our pleasures, speaks in our conscience, but shouts in our pain; it is His megaphone to rouse a deaf world."[16]

Since evil and pain do exist in this world, God sees great utility in them. While He can't be (and shouldn't be) blamed for causing all the pain and evil we suffer from, He will use it to accomplish some residual good. Whether that

---

[16]Lewis. P. 91.

good be in shaping our character, strengthening dependence on the divine, or loosening our heart's grip on a fleeting world (Romans 8:28), God can use our pain for good.

Life is not all pain and heartache. Great beauty, joy and happiness can be found scattered across creation and throughout our lives. God intends such desirables to be a blessing to us, but never a distraction for us. C.S. Lewis draws a timely analogy of life's joys: "Our father refreshes us on the journey with some pleasant inns, but will not encourage us to mistake them for home."[17]

> *Since evil and pain do exist in this present creation, God sees great utility in them.*

---

[17] Ibid. 116.

APPLICATION AND REFLECTION:

When we begin to understand that the evil and pain we experience is a by-product of the much larger problem of living in a morally fallen universe, we realize "Why me?" can be a pretty self-centered question. Knowing that the impact of sin is universal, we should actually expect that we will experience some amount of pain and suffering simply because we live in a fallen world. This is not to say we should have a fatalistic attitude about life. Wise choices can help minimize the pain and disappointment we experience. Thankfully, our fallen universe is also filled with great beauty and everyday joys.

Our view of God as an all-powerful and all-good God shouldn't be challenged by evil in this world. We accept the fact that not only did God not cause evil and pain in the first place, but that His eventual plan is to restore His initial design by creating a new Heaven and new Earth which will be free of evil and pain forever (Revelation 21: 1,4).

1. How can realizing that pain and evil are universal, help reduce our own internal struggle when bad things happen to us or to those we love?
2. How does God's just and loving nature demand that He also judge evil in the world? Would He be loving and just if He just "let it slide?"
3. Re-read the closing C.S. Lewis quote at the end of the chapter. How is the thought "we are not home yet" comforting in the face of pain?

CHAPTER THREE INTRODUCTION:

CHAPTER THREE: God answers prayer.

"Therefore I have declared that which I did not understand, things too wonderful for me, which I did not know." Job 42:3

"For as the heavens are higher than the Earth, so are my ways higher than your ways and my thoughts than your thoughts." Isaiah 55:9

The Bible teaches and records hundreds of examples of God answering prayer. He blessed infertile Abraham and Sarah with a baby boy after a lifetime of longing; he was 100, and she was 90 (Genesis 21). He answered King Hezekiah's prayer for military victory over the Assyrians (2 Kings 19). Jesus answered the plea of panicked parents and healed their terminally ill daughter (Luke 8). The list could go on and on.

Still today, many of our prayers seem to go unanswered. If we consider only prayers answered exactly as asked, it can cast doubt on our prayer life, on ourselves, and even on God. As we try to understand God's response to our sincere prayers, we must harmonize all of scripture. Consider David's struggle reflected in prayer in Psalm 10:1 *"Why do you stand afar off, O Lord? Why do you hide yourself in times of trouble?"* Our trust in God in times of trouble can increase if we realize the many ways that God answers prayer, and if we don't limit Him by our own expectations.

CHAPTER THREE: God Answers Prayer.

The title to this book asks three questions:

>1. God, where are you?
>
>2. Why do bad things happen?
>
>3. Why do prayers go unanswered?

This chapter considers the question "Why do prayers go unanswered?" We ask this when we feel no answers seem to come in response to our prayers. This chapter will suggest that a more correct wording of this soul-wrenching question would be "Why do prayers *seem* to go unanswered?"

When King David's faith was tested, like us, he too wondered if God had turned His back on him. He felt like God disregarded his prayer (see Psalm 10:1 quoted in the chapter introduction). David first penned the words that Christ Himself would later quote on the cross *"My God, my God, why have you forsaken me?"* (Psalm 22:1).

Faith can feel like a roller coaster. David went through times of great uncertainty, he also displayed times of assurance. While he had times of doubt, David's underlying belief was that God would not permanently abandoned him or turn a deaf ear to his cries. He later declares in Psalm 37:28 *"For the Lord loves justice, and does not forsake His godly ones..."* It is clear to say that David had times when he genuinely felt his prayers were "falling on deaf or uninterested ears." But a thorough examination of scripture shows us this was not the case then, nor is it for us now. God does hear and answer prayer.

As David confidently said, and this book concurs:

"But as for me, my prayer is to thee, O Lord, at an acceptable time; O God in the greatness of thy loving-kindness, answer me with thy saving truth" Psalm 69:13.

This verse in Psalms as well as other chapters on prayer, like Psalm 86, reveal David's confidence that God would answer prayer. When we examine David's prayer life, we find that David often didn't dictate what God must do in response to his prayers. While at times David did make specific requests, David often simply cried out to God in his distress simply seeking whatever relief God deemed best.

> *Faith can feel like a roller coaster. King David went through times of great uncertainty, he also displayed times of assurance.*

We often mistakenly think God hasn't answered or heard our prayers because He didn't fulfill our request how or when we wanted it. This typically causes either doubt or guilt toward ourselves or God. However, if we realize the many ways God answers prayer, we need seldom wonder why prayers seemingly go unanswered. Consider some of the variety of ways God does answer our prayers:

"Yes!" We love it when our prayers are answered exactly as requested. We got the job. We're healed. The need is met. The answer unfolds in our lives. Of all God's responses to our prayers, this is understandably our favorite.

"Not yet." Many times God has an answer on the way, but the timing isn't right. Habakkuk 2:3 reminds us: *"The vision is yet for the appointed time…it will not fail. Though it tarries, wait for it."* The more desperate our need, the less we like to wait. If we aren't careful, we can mistakenly assume that no answer now means no answer ever (see Saul's dreadful, impatient disobedience in 1 Samuel 13).

Be patient. Your inability to see an answer does not mean one isn't there or on the way. Learn to wait, and learn what the time of waiting is meant to teach you.

It is easier to be patient if we keep in mind that God's long term interest is in His creatures living an abundant life (John 10:10) in the midst of a fallen universe, while becoming a redeemed and contagious representation of His righteousness.

Someday we will be restored to our unfallen intended glory in God's presence forever in a new Heaven and a new Earth (Revelation 21:1) untainted by evil, unfamiliar with even the concept of pain." Someday isn't yet, and we must learn to wait.

"No." As much as we don't like to wait for answers to prayer, the answer we like to receive even less from God is "no." God isn't an enabling parent and He will say no when necessary. Moses wasn't allowed in the Promised Land.

God said no to David's desire to build the temple. Paul did not receive the healing he prayed for.

God will sometimes tell you no. Listen, discern, trust and accept it.

"I'm doing something different." As Isaiah 55:8, 9 tells us, God's understanding, solutions, and plans are infinitely higher and greater than ours (see chapter introduction). If we choose to be less in the habit of telling God what to do, and more in the habit of simply making our needs known, we will be more likely to see and celebrate answers to prayer we didn't anticipate. How often have we missed being thankful and growing in our faith because we missed noticing an answer to prayer we didn't expect?

> *How often have we missed being thankful and growing in our faith because we missed noticing an answer to prayer we didn't expect?*

Country singer Garth Brooks had a hit song that said, "Sometimes I thank God for unanswered prayers." The point of the song was that unanswered prayers are often simply prayers that God is addressing in unanticipated ways. At other times, our prayers really aren't best for us, and God loves us too much to grant our demands.

The prophet Isaiah's words cause us to wonder how often the directives and expectations that we deliver in the form of prayers cause us to miss His creative new plans:

"Do not call to mind the former things, nor ponder things of the past. Behold I will do something new, now it will spring forth, and will you not be aware of it?" I will even make a roadway in the wilderness and rivers in the desert" Isaiah 43:18, 19.

"I'm doing something you aren't aware of." The story in 2 Kings 7 is a perfect example of God doing something His people didn't realize. In this story, the enemy Arameans had come to destroy Israel. The Israelites were crying out in fear of an attack by their enemies camped outside the city. One night, miraculously and unknown to the Israelites, God drove the Arameans away. They fled in fear, leaving all their possessions behind.

> *What might God be doing in your life that you don't see or anticipate?*

Four leprous men who were hiding just outside the city decided to investigate. They discovered the unexpected work of God and passed the news along to an unsuspecting Jewish people inside the city walls. A party broke out in place of their panic! While they were fearing for their lives, God was working another unexpected plan for their good.

What might God be doing in your life that you don't see or anticipate? Ask Him to open the eyes of your heart, so you will be able to recognize, respond, and rejoice in what He is doing.

There are certainly other ways God answers prayer than the few mentioned here. The ways listed of how God answers our prayers is not meant to suggest that we don't pray or tell God our needs. As with all our beliefs, to understand prayer we must seek to harmonize scripture. While David often cried out to God without specific requests, James 4:2 tells us *"You do not have because you do not ask."*

In light of this, ask passionately. Ask often. Ask in faith. Expect God to hear and to answer your prayers in a variety of ways. Model the attitude of Jesus. In His most desperate prayer in the garden of Gethsemane, even though He asked specifically to be relieved of the responsibility of the cross, He yielded His desires to our Heavenly Father by concluding His prayer with *"Nevertheless, not my will, but yours be done"* (Matthew 26:39).

God wants to work in your life. God is working in your life. He wants you to eventually recognize and acknowledge this. *"Be cheerful no matter what; pray all the time; Thank God no matter what happens. This is the way God wants you who belong to Christ Jesus to live"* (1 Thessalonians 5:16-18, The Message).

APPLICATION AND REFLECTION:

Just because God hasn't answered your prayers the way you've asked, doesn't mean He doesn't care, or won't respond. In fact, we can miss answers to prayers simply because God responded in a way we didn't ask or think of.

This chapter has identified several alternative ways God answers our prayers:

1. Yes!
2. Not yet.
3. No.
4. I'm doing something different than what you have asked for.
5. An answer is on the way and you don't even realize it.

God's ways are higher and better than our ways, and Ephesians 3: 20 tells us He does abundantly beyond what we can ask or think of! There is an old saying, "You can't see the forest for the trees." The implication is that sometimes we miss what we are searching for, even though it is right in front of us.

1. Think back over your life. If you've ever asked God for anything, try to find an example of each kind of the five listed answers from Him to your prayers.
2. Say five prayers of thanks, out loud, for each answer you were able to identify. Even "No" from God is better than us forcing our will onto God in prayer.

CHAPTER INTRODUCTION:

CHAPTER FOUR: Really bad spiritual advice about why bad things happen.

"Job answered: 'How long are you going to keep battering away at me, pounding me with these harangues? Time after time you jump all over me. Do you have no conscience, abusing me like this? Even if I have, somehow or other, gotten off track, what business is that of yours? Why do you insist on putting me down, using my troubles as a stick to beat me? Tell it to God-He's the one behind all this, He's the one who dragged me into this mess'" (Job 19: 1-6, The Message).

> Most of us have had people say something to us in difficult times that didn't help. People who offer such remarks are usually well-intentioned. Perhaps they were trying to comfort or console us. Perhaps they were trying to let us know we aren't alone and they understand how we feel. At other times, people say things that are mean-spirited in the midst of our struggles.
>
> Job had three "friends" who visited him under the pretense of comforting him. However, the conversation soon went badly. The comforters adopted an air of condescending self-righteousness that belittled Job and added internal anguish to his physical and emotional pain. Perhaps you'll recognize some of the timeless bad advice and unhealthy perspectives they tried to share with him.

CHAPTER FOUR: Really bad spiritual advice about why bad things happen

We try our best to cope when disappointment, tragedy, heartache or pain strike. Part of coping is to "make sense" of what happened. In our quest for understanding, to relieve anxiety and try to gain control, we ask questions: *"What happened? How did it happen? Why did it happen? Who was involved? What does it mean? What now? Do I somehow deserve this?"*

Job could have easily asked a host of questions trying to figure out what happened to him, and why. Poor Job; he had done nothing to deserve one of the greatest *personal* tragedies ever recorded. He was not devastated as part of an international war, genocide, or by any choices he made. He wasn't one of countless people impacted by a widespread natural disaster. Job's was a personal catastrophe, of enormous proportions. He was thoroughly devastated. Job's tragedy struck his children, his marriage, his wealth, his identity and his health.

> *In our quiet, honest moments the unanticipated, unknown potential future realities of life leave us feeling vulnerable.*

It scares us that the same God who we pray to for protection is the God who gave permission for this whole devastation to happen! In small ways we identify with Job.

All of us have experienced pain, ridicule, loss or unjust suffering in some way or another.

As human beings we like a certain level of control over what happens in our lives. We usually enjoy surprises, but we certainly would like to do without unexpected, undesired experiences. In our quiet, honest moments the unanticipated, unknown potential future realities of life leave us feeling vulnerable. We wonder which phone call, text, meeting with the boss or doctor's appointment will be the one bearing news we hoped would never apply to us or to those we love?

> *Really bad theology does not make really bad experiences any more manageable.*

Thankfully we escape such tragedies most of the time, but it only took two horrendous unexpected days which were totally out of Job's control to ruin his entire life as he knew it. Job provides a lasting reminder of the fragile and vulnerable nature of life.

When tragedy strikes, we are a lot like Job. If we can at least gain some understanding of what is going on, it tends to alleviate some of our anxiety. Not knowing or understanding exacerbates our fears, and our feelings of vulnerability can grow rather than subside. No one likes sustained and increasing fear. In the face of pain, evil, heartache or disappointment we are desperate to understand.

Knowing the how what and why of something happening helps us in several ways:

A. How do I respond to minimize negative consequences and return to normal as soon as possible?
B. How can I avoid this from ever happening again in the future?
C. Who is responsible for this? (Who is to blame?)
D. How do I regain "control" of my/our life?

Thankfully, knowing "How, who and why?" can indeed be helpful in defining appropriate responses: What is the correct medical treatment plan? How do I repair the damage? Do we call the insurance company? Can the issue be resolved and the relationship repaired?

> *The more devastating the pain, the fewer words will be found to help. "Compassionate presence" is often the best comfort to a suffering body and soul.*

Likewise, we can usually learn from painful events and often figure out how recurrences can at least be minimized if not altogether avoided in the future. Wisdom and common sense can turn many painful experiences into valuable protective lessons for next time. Many of life's negative experiences can be avoided, or at least greatly minimized. Much of what can't be avoided can at least be learned from for future benefit.

For example: One way to avoid getting into another brawl with a drunken bar patron (that ended up getting you shot at, arrested and thrown in jail) would be to decide to never go to a bar again. This is sound logic based on the simple truth: A person will never get shot at by a drunk in a bar if that person never goes to a bar in the first place.

Our desire to understand, to figure out, and hopefully control and avoid future pain and heartache is what motivates us to explain and label why bad things happen to good people, and why prayers seem to go unanswered. Not only do victims try to figure things out, strangers, by-passers and close friends often try to process and explain the causes of our pain, disappointments, and heartaches.

> *Basically, Eliphaz is saying "Job, somehow God has killed your children, destroyed all your wealth and smitten you with a dreadful disease, and the reason God has done this is obviously because you have done something to deserve it."*

Ask anyone who has come close to a "Job-like day" and they will concur; when significantly bad things happen, people offer explanations as to why. Unfortunately, such explanations are often unsolicited! Whether a career crashed, a loved one died or we were the victim of a horrible evil, people offer reasons. Many of their explanations often do little to help victims cope; some do more harm than good.

Many survivors find no comfort when told "Everything happens for a reason." Grief is seldom diminished when told "At least they are in a better place." People lost and isolated in their pain feel no solace when told "I know how you feel; you'll get over it."

Bad explanations and responses to tragedy, evil, and pain can be made worse when they are "spiritualized." Many well-meaning people try to explain the unexplainable by mixing God or the Bible into the equation. Really bad theology does not make really bad experiences any more manageable.

> *Job's friends argued that both the good and bad in life are dispensed according to what we deserve based on what we've done and the condition or our hearts.*

Perhaps no one knows this better than Job. Shortly after devastation struck Job, three friends of his, Eliphaz, Bildad, and Zophar, *"made an appointment to come to sympathize with him and comfort him"* (Job 2:11).

Aware of Job's loss of family, wealth and health his three friends approached Job. The Bible says they were so shocked by his hideous appearance that they tore their robes and threw dust in the air over their heads. This was the culturally common expression of intense grief. Seeing that *"His pain was very great,"* (physical as well as emotional) Job's friends sat in silence for a solid week (Job 2: 11-13). Up to this point, their responses were appropriate. The more devastating the pain, the fewer words will be found to help. A compassionate presence is often the best comfort to a wounded body and soul.

Unfortunately, Job's friends didn't stop there. The next thirty chapters of Job chronicle the conversational debate between Job and his friends. In this exchange we see Job reeling in spiritual disequilibrium, trying desperately to reconcile what happened in light of who he believed God to be and how he believed God worked. He also spent great effort trying to defend himself against the accusatory and bad theological explanations and "comforting remarks" of his friends.

The comments of Job's three friends along with Elihu, a young bystander to the conversation, fall into two basic lines of thinking: First, Godly people prosper. Good things happen to good people who do good things. Second, the inverse is also true: Wicked people suffer. Bad things happen to bad people who do bad things. Job's friends argued that both the good and bad in life are dispensed according to what we deserve based on what we've done and the condition of our hearts.

Eliphaz eloquently makes the argument that the other three debating friends will champion. He begins by speaking in a manipulative way: *"If one ventures a word with you, will you become impatient?"* (Job 4: 2). Eliphaz was basically saying "Job, do you mind if I give you some advice, or are you just going to get defensive if I tell you something you don't want to hear?"

Not waiting for Job's permission to speak, Eliphaz launched his advice and holds nothing back:

> *"Your words have helped the tottering to stand and you have strengthened feeble knees. But now it has come to you, and you are impatient; it touches you and you are dismayed."* (Job 4: 4, 5).

The crux of his "comforting" argument is found in verse 7: *"according to what I have seen, those who plow iniquity and those who sow trouble, harvest it."* In other words, "Job you aren't as good and holy as you appear or want us to believe. Job, you have obviously done something to deserve this." Eliphaz pummels Job further in the next verses attributing all Job's heartache to the work of God: *"By the breath of God they (wicked, judgment-deserving people) perish, and by the blast of His anger they come to an end"* (Job 4: 9).

> *Bad theology works for those it serves. We choose to believe it because it supports the world-view we prefer.*

Eliphaz provides an age-old summary of a theology of the earthly prosperity of the righteous in Job 5: 20-27:

A. God protects righteous people from famine.
B. God delivers good people from the sword.

C. No one will gossip about righteous people, or at least gossip won't hurt you.
D. Violence is no concern for good people.
E. Wild beasts will never hurt the righteous.
F. The righteous are crime free.
G. Good people don't struggle with infertility.
H. Righteous people die at an old age of natural causes.

> *If the righteous are blessed and the wicked are not, then why do so many good things happen to ungodly people? Certainly there are many healthy, wealthy and relatively happy people who have no belief or interest in God whatsoever. Likewise, many Godly people suffer all over the world.*

In light of these truths, Eliphaz admonishes Job to seek God in order to discern why he deserves this pain and tells Job to be happy for this divine, devastating 'spanking' of sorts: *"Do not despise the discipline of the almighty. For He inflicts pain and gives relief."* (Job 5: 17, 18).

Basically, Eliphaz made the point "Job, somehow God has killed your children, destroyed all your wealth and smitten you with a dreadful disease. The reason God has done this is obviously because you have done something to deserve it." This explanation is the downward side of "everything happens for a reason." This carries with it the assumption if bad things happen, you either did something to deserve it, or God has some reason for it that you just don't understand. It is not a comforting perspective in the midst of unexpected pain. Such "comfort" causes us to doubt our view of ourselves and to doubt who God is and how He must see us; it can help make us spiritually and emotionally paranoid.

> *Job's friends are not only heartless in their "comforting confrontations" they are relentless. Until the dialogue ceases in the final rs, the book of Job becomes an accusatory and unkind diatribe by his friends.*

Today this mindset is often labelled "prosperity theology." Until bad things happen, it is nice to think that all the good things that are happening to me are because somehow I deserve it, due to God's goodness and my inherent goodness and personal obedience. The problem with such theology is it does little to accurately describe life. If the righteous are blessed and the wicked are not, then why do so many good things happen to ungodly people? Certainly there are many healthy, wealthy, and relatively happy people who have no belief or interest in God whatsoever. Likewise, many Godly people suffer all over the world. How does prosperity theology fit them? Do we dare assert that starving believers in third world poverty just don't have enough faith, or those Christians killed in some atrocious genocide somehow deserved it and we do not?

Bildad tells Job if he were the pure and righteous person he claimed to be (and they believed him) *"Surely now God would arouse Himself for you and restore your righteous estate"* (Job 8: 6). Verse 20 of the same chapter strikes with the judgmental double-edge of *"God will not reject a man of integrity, nor will he support evildoers."*

Repeatedly Job's friends offer their bad theological consolations. Their ongoing theme is bad things don't happen to good people. If bad things do happen, they are short lived, God stops and undoes it quickly.

Zophar joins the "pile on" by telling Job if he would just humble himself and acknowledge his obvious (yet not observable) sin, God would fix everything: *"Your life would be brighter than noonday; darkness would be like the morning"* (Job 11: 17). In Chapter 19 Job tries to push-back on Bildad's second attack, and the ongoing onslaught from his friends:

> *"Job answered: 'How long are you going to keep battering away at me, pounding me with these harangues? Time after time after time you jump all over me. Do you have no conscience, abusing me like this? Even if I have, somehow or other, gotten off track, what business is that of yours? Why do you insist on putting me down, using my troubles as a stick to beat me? Tell it to God-He's the one behind all this, He's the one who dragged me into this mess."* (Job 19: 1-6, The Message).

Job's friends are not only heartless in their "comforting confrontations" they are relentless. Until the dialogue ceases in the final chapters, the book of Job becomes an accusatory and unkind diatribe by his friends. This is exemplified in Zophar's second set of comments beginning in chapter 20.

> *Their ongoing theme is bad things don't happen to good people. If bad things do happen, they are short lived, God stops and undoes it quickly.*

Zophar vents his offense, telling Job *"I can't believe what I'm hearing...how dare you insult my intelligence like this! Well here's a piece of my mind!"* (Job 20: 1, 3, The Message). Zophar proceeds to again bombard Job with the idea that God eventually punishes evil doers. To Zophar, Job obviously fell into this category. Job's blessed and prosperous life was short lived and obviously a wicked one:

"The increase of the house of the wicked will depart, his possessions will flow away. In the day of His anger, this is the wicked man's portion from God. Even the heritage decreed to him by God" (Job 20: 28, 29).

The good thing about bad theology like this is that at least there are answers! It is less unnerving to believe that we basically get what we deserve (always and eventually) than to think we live in a universe that isn't fair. The truth in our universe is the reverse of Prosperity theology; bad things can (and do) happen to good, underserving people (and vice-versa).

Bad theology works for those it serves. We choose to believe it because it supports the world-view we prefer. In Job's case his friends liked the idea they could guarantee good things would happen in life by being good; they could also guarantee that bad things wouldn't happen as long as they didn't do bad things to deserve punishment.

The difficulty comes when we try to explain and cope with the reality that bad things often happen to good people who did nothing to deserve it. If God governs the universe in a simple cause-effect mode, the pain in life is disillusioning.

> *The truth in our universe is the reverse of "Prosperity theology:" Bad things can (and do) happen to good, underserving people (and vice-versa).*

There are many people today who use discomforting words similar to the line of reasoning found among Job's friends. They mean well. For many, their remarks can be summarized in a popular statement, "Everything happens for a reason." The next chapter deals with this line of thought and the fact that for many sincere suffering people more questions are raised than answered.

APPLICATION AND REFLECTION:

It would be nice if only good things happened to good people, and vice-versa. However, life on this planet isn't that way. People get what they don't "deserve" all the time. Really nice, good, decent people often live through terrible pain or disappointment. Likewise, people who seem self-centered and unguided by any moral compass of good can experience wealth, health, and happiness they don't seem to deserve.

"Prosperity theology" only truly works when life is going well and hopes and dreams are becoming reality on a regular basis, amidst a healthy and comfortable life. While God does bless obedience (Luke 6: 38), Jesus also promises "tribulation" in our lives (John 16: 33). We simply cannot guarantee all good or bad in anyone's earthly life. Someday, in Heaven, we will no longer know evil or pain but not until that day.

1. There are general laws of "sowing and reaping." Galatians 6: 7 tells us *"Whatsoever a man sows that shall he also reap."* Good deeds do typically have good results, and vice-versa. However, this is not an iron-clad guarantee. Why do you suppose people struggle when things happen that they "don't deserve?"

2. Where does our innate desire for life to be "fair" come from? How might this be a part of God's nature of an inherent sense of justice, reflected in us?

CHAPTER INTRODUCTION

CHAPTER FIVE: "Everything happens for a reason."

"Remember now, whoever perished being innocent? Or where were the upright destroyed? According to what I have seen, those who plow iniquity and those who sow trouble harvest it...as for me, I would seek God, and I would place my cause before God" (Job 4: 7,9; 5: 8).

Job's friends applied a sort of divine cause-effect understanding of the universe to make sense of his pain

A common catch-phrase applied to a variety of pain, struggle and disappointment in life is "Everything happens for a reason." At times, this thought can be somewhat comforting. When we experience significant loss or hardship, there can be some consolation that our loss or suffering was not in vain, as though there is some "higher purpose" served by our pain.

Depending on the degree of pain, suffering or injustice endured, this remark can go from comforting to disheartening. The claim that "Everything happens for a reason" alludes to some grand design that God Himself is orchestrating together for good, and it implies He simply needed some of your pain and suffering to finish the job.

CHAPTER FIVE: "Everything happens for a reason."

People who claim "everything happens for a reason" are typically suggesting that God causes all things to occur according to some often hidden divine master plan.

Simply put: Our understanding is human and limited. We may only see abuse, physical suffering, death, loss or injustice; don't worry, some day you will see God's strategy and you will have a divine "A-HA!" moment and the larger purpose and reason God did/caused such horrible things to happen will finally spring into view and make sense.

> *Depending on the degree of pain, suffering or injustice endured, this remark can go from comforting to disheartening.*

This is main-stream theology for many. One famous contemporary Christian author put it this way (Note: this author will not be cited, to protect confidentiality):

> "Every disappointment even if tragic and evil is His appointment. I may not like God's appointment or agree with it, but God is in charge. Nothing happens apart from His permission. **God is the ultimate authority, the ultimate cause; He has the ultimate responsibility for all that goes on.** That's why He commands us in everything give thanks for this is God's will for you in Christ Jesus. What possible

reason could there be to give thanks in everything if God isn't sovereign. Why should we thank Him if He isn't responsible, if He's not in control?"

The unspoken implication is the same as with Job's friends: "You don't know or understand why this horrible tragedy has come upon you, but God has some great undisclosed reason why He orchestrated it." The problem with bad theology and bad explanations is they "work" just enough to go unquestioned and to be repeatedly used. Let's consider the following scenario:

You are at a family cookout and your uncle passes out unexpectedly. He's rushed to the Emergency Room. While his fainting spell was just due to too much heat and too little water, upon check-in, his high blood pressure lead the ER doctors to discover a heart blockage. About the time he should have been eating a grilled burger, he's having life-saving triple bypass surgery.

> *We like a God who looks out for us like that, who compensates for our behavior and saves us even when we don't realize it.*

Later that evening, a family member muses out loud about uncle's untimely fainting spell that may have saved his life and says, "Everything happens for a reason." The unspoken implication is since God couldn't reach your uncle by text or email to warn him of his condition, and because uncle disregarded any exercise and ate unhealthy for most of his life, God orchestrated the fainting spell to get him on the cardiac surgeon's table.

God is good, and certainly everything...even this picnic-interrupting fainting spell "happens for a reason."

In this scenario, the thought that God went to great lengths to orchestrate life-saving unrelated events as part of His master plan is rather comforting. We like a God who looks out for us like that, who compensates for our behavior and saves us even when we don't realize it.

This book is not questioning that this scenario isn't totally possible. God could very well have used a fainting spell to save your uncle's life. But how would the explanation get more difficult if your uncle would have died in the E.R.? Suddenly "everything happens for a reason" leaves us in unresolved suspense. "O.K., uncle died for a reason...but will we ever know it? Will we have to wait until heaven to discover God's "reason" for ruining the cookout, devastating your aunt and cousins with grief, and 'taking' your uncle?

> *"Everything happens for a reason" alludes to some grand-design that God Himself is orchestrating together for good, and it implies He simply needed some of your pain and suffering to finish the job.*

For the sake of illustration, let's complicate this scenario even more. Let's say at the cookout you learned a variety of horrible family happenings:

1. A cousin was just diagnosed with late-stage breast cancer. The doctors give her three months to live, and she'll leave behind three children ages 18 months to 7 years old. How does "Everything happens for a reason" seem to help?
2. Another family member is heartbroken, scared and furious. She just discovered her 6 year old daughter was repeatedly molested by a neighbor. She asks "How God could let this happen to our little girl, what do we do for her now?" How does "Everything happens for a reason" address the horrors of this child and her parent's nightmare?
3. Another cousin wonders what to tell his best friend (both are Christians). His friend who was driving home from his first day of an exciting new job was struck by a hit-and-run drunk driver and now doctors don't think he'll ever walk again. How can "Everything happens for a reason" possibly comfort this friend?

When such well-meaning Christians are questioned for the theological basis of "Everything happens for a reason" they often have no reply. It just feels reassuring, and they know they heard it somewhere before.

To be fair, this position is popular and can be Biblically supported to some degree. The Bible is full of accounts of God choosing to direct the course of human events. Likewise, poetic statements like Psalm 149: 16 are popularly referenced when defending this view:

> *"Thine eyes have seen my unformed substance; in thy book they were written, the days that were*

ordained for me, when as yet there was not one of them."

A popular theological term behind "everything happens for a reason" is predestination. Predestination means that God pre-destines the outcomes of every moment of our lives and every action and activity of each pre-ordained day. Verses like Romans 8:28-30 are referenced in support of this meticulous control God exercises over the entire universe:

> *To justify our inability to make sense out of such apparent cruelty, do we really help matters by excusing God's silence and our wondering anguish with a simple and resigning "Everything happens for a reason"?*

> "And we know that God causes all things to work together for good to those who love God, to those who are called according to His purpose. For whom He foreknew, He also predestined to become conformed to the image of His Son...and whom He predestined, these He also called; and whom He called, these He also justified; and whom He justified, these He also glorified."

This book certainly upholds the ultimate supremacy of God. God is all-powerful (1 Chronicles 29: 11). God is all knowing and wise (Romans 11: 33-36). God is ever-present (Psalm 139: 7-10). The providence of God sustains and is supreme over His creation (Colossians 1: 15-18). Providence is understood as "God omnisciently directing the universe and the affairs of humankind with wise benevolence."[18]

The phrase "Everything happens for a reason" begs a question about providence. What does it truly mean? Must God *cause* all things in order to be all-powerful? How can He cause all things, even evil things, if He is all-good?

This common phrase also begs a question regarding the resourcefulness of God. Is there no other way for an all-powerful and all-loving God to accomplish His plans other than to "take" your uncle, or "appoint" your niece to be sexually abused? Must God afflict your nice cousin with breast cancer or pre-destine a young Christian man to spend the rest of his days in a wheelchair?

> *Is God's total ability equal to His total responsibility?*

Are we certain this same God, who created the universe from nothing ages ago by His unimaginable power and creativity, can now only accomplish His agenda through causing the torturous pain and abuse of the very creatures He made and loves? Must God be the cause of evil and pain? To justify our inability to make sense out of such apparent cruelty, do we really help matters by excusing

---

[18] Dictionary.com

God's silence and our wondering anguish with a simple and resigning everything happens for a reason?

Consider the implications of "Everything happens for a reason." Since God is capable of doing whatever He chooses does it mean that every act and event under the sun is His doing? Is God's total ability equal to His total responsibility?

> *Everything happens because of one or more reasons. These reasons are not necessarily what God would have planned or chosen for His creation, but He is no less providential.*

This very statement begs a larger question: "Is God indeed capable of doing whatever He chooses?" The perfect goodness of God would suggest that there are some things God cannot do, or perhaps God simply cannot choose to do: God cannot act unjustly. God cannot be untruthful. God cannot act unloving. To do any of these would be against His perfectly just, true and loving nature. The one thing (or set of actions) God is incapable of is to act inconsistent with His divine perfect nature (Titus 1: 2; James 1: 13). God cannot act inconsistent with who He is. God is incapable of random or premeditated acts of injustice, abuse or deception.

While God is incapable of such deeds, the universe seems full of random and premeditated acts of abuse, injustice, and deception. Those holding God responsible as the cause for everything offer the previously mentioned

"Everything happens for a reason" and shrug off responsibility of addressing the question: "What possible reason could God have for doing that?"

While the Bible does speak of what theologians refer to as the "pre-ordained will of God" (providence), other verses speak in what could be seen as contradictory ways. Passages like Jeremiah 19:5 seem to indicate some things happen totally outside of God's doing. In fact, in this verse, God says that the horrendous act of child sacrifice by fire didn't even cross His mind:

> *Those holding God responsible as the cause for everything offer the previously mentioned "Everything happens for a reason" and shrug off responsibility of addressing the question: "What possible reason could God have for doing that?"*

"(The people of Judah)...have built the high places of Baal to burn their (infant) sons in the fire as burnt offerings. A thing which I never commanded, or spoke of, nor did it ever enter my mind."

How would an Old Testament observer explain "Everything happens for a reason" in this gruesome context, as though God had some unknown reason for child sacrifice? Especially when God is saying He never commanded it, and it never crossed His mind?

There are also an abundance of passages that seem to put the consequences of actions squarely on the shoulders of humans and the choices they have made. For example, in the opening chapter of the book of Proverbs Solomon instructs his son about personal responsibility. It is a matter of choice to either heed or deny truth and bear the good (or bad) consequences of what we choose. To Solomon, the reason much happens "for a reason" is not God's direct and premeditated execution of a master plan. For Solomon, many things often happen as a result of wise, simple or foolish human decisions (Proverbs 1-31).

> *For those who find "Everything happens for a reason" as an inadequate catch-all response to the horrors of life...consider there may be as many as four or more possible reasons why everything happens...*

When passages of scripture seem to contradict each other, the answer is not to discard the Bible or over-rule one passage for the sake of another. Discerning Christians must seek to wisely harmonize scriptures in order to find as non-contradictory and complete an interpretation of the Bible as possible.

This book is in indirect agreement that "Everything happens for a reason." However, the implied "reason" is not always a hidden or grandiose part of God's pre-determined master plan. The position of this book is more accurately stated "Everything happens because of one or more reasons. These reasons are not necessarily what God would have planned or chosen for His creation, but He is no less providential."

For those who find "Everything happens for a reason" as an inadequate catch-all response to the horrors of life, and to those unable to imply that God actually orchestrates (appoints) all abuse, suffering, injustice and disappointment in the universe for divine reasons we just can't understand, consider there may be as many as four or more possible reasons why everything happens, and especially why bad things happen and prayers don't get answered.

This suggested broader Biblically based understanding of causality in the universe helps sort out the "why" behind the happenings of life. This book suggests four possible causes to the good and bad in life. The next chapter attempts to unpack this perspective.

APPLICATION AND REFLECTION:

Contrary to the statement confronted in this chapter, what if everything DOESN'T happen for a reason? What if this universe is irreparably damaged by evil and we simply can't control or avoid a certain amount of heartache and suffering, no matter what we do or believe?

Actually, this isn't far from how we live most of our lives. None of us labor over whether God wants us to order lemon in our ice water or drink it plain.

Unless God is obsessively and compulsively in charge of EVERY action by EVERY person, animal, plant, tree etc. in the universe, we must live with the reality that much of what happens may not be part of some premeditated divine minutely detailed directive. Does God have a plan? ABSOLUTELY! Just read the Bible from Genesis to Revelation and you'll discover His amazing, grace-filled and detailed plan to redeem humanity. This plan is simply not an all-or-nothing approach to why events happen in the universe.

1. God created His universe. Much of what happens is due to how God created in the first place. Gravity and free will are just two causes behind much of what occurs. How is this a comfort in dealing with the pain and suffering in life?

2. How might we feel more vulnerable if we accept that much of life is not a direct order by God? How does this raise our level of personal responsibility?

CHAPTER INTRODUCTION

CHAPTER SIX: Four causes for everything.

"Therefore I have declared that which I did not understand, Things too wonderful for me, which I did not know" (Job 42: 3)

> After all of the debating between Job and his companions, they found no conclusive reason for why tragedy happens. As hard as we search for the "why" behind some of our worst experiences, we often meet an unyielding silence of understanding.
>
> Many things that happen in life don't make sense. Much happens that is undeserved, both good and bad, and there seems to be no reason God would have approved or denied such occurrences.
>
> This chapter broadens the possible answers to "why." Do we have to blame God? Perhaps it is possible to not lessen God's sovereignty, while at the same time removing some of the causality from God's direct responsibility.
>
> This is done by seeking to describe four Biblically compatible reasons for "why" things might happen. This paradigm attempts to give a broader base of understanding and place of faith from which to respond to and process life.

CHAPTER SIX: Four causes for everything.

God is all-powerful and all-loving and He is capable of anything He chooses. However, consider four possible "causes" for everything rather than the default that God did it and what we can't comprehend falls in the category of "Everything happens for a reason."

First, God obviously exercises control in this world. "He changes the times and the seasons...He removes kings and establishes kings..." (Daniel 2: 21). God is an all-powerful God and He is active in his creation. God directly causes many things.

Many things that happen God indirectly causes as a result of the laws and dynamics God has established to sustain His creation. This includes everything from how weather patterns function to the ever-present force of gravity.

Second, much of life is a result of the fallen condition of the planet we live on. Sin brought death and disease to Earth. As such, a good deal of our suffering is simply a by-product of the destruction of sin.

Third, Human choice is responsible for an overwhelming amount of what happens. Good, Godly choices typically yield good results, and vice-versa. Still, it is not guaranteed that bad brings bad, and good always yields good.

Finally, Satan has a will and a plan to destroy or at least damage all God has created for good. Many victims will find no answer to why some great evil happened to them other than someone yielded to sinful temptation and chose to commit such a sin at their expense. On apparently rare occasions, Satan has direct permission to afflict us as well.

Let's consider in greater detail these four possible "causes" for everything. This Biblically based perspective can help us develop a broader understanding for why things happen, and perhaps "blame" God less, and trust Him more.

The first cause is God. God indeed is the "prime mover" ancient philosophers mused about. As noted throughout the book of Job, God directly and indirectly causes much of what happens in the universe. The long list of God's activity includes the following: He *creates* (Genesis 1:1). God *commands nature*, as in parting the Red Sea (Exodus 19). God *protects* (Psalm 121). God *smites in judgment* with physical affliction (2 Chronicles 26: 19, 20). God *punishes* with the elements like an earthquake, tornado or forest fire (Isaiah 29: 6). God *heals* (Psalm 103). God comforts (2 Corinthians 1). God *forgives* (1 John 1:9).

> *God's wisdom is not, and never was pledged to keep a fallen world happy, or to make loneliness comfortable.*

God does so many amazing, awe-inspiring, joy-inciting, and sobering things. God has the power to do as He chooses, and He is active in His creation, *He is the direct cause of much of what happens.* Often God's activity is in response to good or evil in the form of a blessing or a curse. God directly provided food in the wilderness for starving Israelites. God destroyed Sodom and Gomorrah for unrepentant sins. God made David King of Israel. God sent His son Jesus Christ to die for and forgive the sins of the world. Throughout history and today, God is the direct cause of much that happens.

God often does use and cause both good and bad things to happen in the cosmic war raging between good and evil. He wants to sufficiently reveal Himself so humanity can choose to follow Him and His will.

God is active in His creation to accomplish His larger eternal purposes, and the ultimate outcome of this struggle has indeed been pre-determined. Someday God will destroy and banish evil forever (Revelation 20). Someday God will restore His original intentions of a righteous creation by establishing a new Heaven and a new Earth (Revelation 21). As explained earlier, this battle pits the force of eternal life (Zoe) emanating from God, against the force of sin, emanating from Satan.

The ultimate stakes of this battle are the souls of humanity. God has gone to great lengths to provide victory in this struggle to every person who will choose it:

> *"For God so loved the world that He gave His only begotten Son, that whoever believes in Him would not perish, but have eternal life"* (John 3: 16).

In this battle, *"It is not God's will for any to perish, but for all to come to repentance"* (2 Peter 3: 9).

God's goal in this struggle is not only for the eventual salvation of mankind someday in Heaven; God also desires for believers to live a transformational life now. While on Earth, we are to increasingly overcome sin and reflect the character and mission of Jesus in ourselves (Philippians 1: 6).

At times, this transformation process is a journey of going through trying times. God often uses hardship to test us and complete us:

> *"Consider it all joy, my brethren, when you encounter various trials, knowing that the testing of your faith produces endurance. And let endurance have its perfect result, that you may be perfect and complete lacking in nothing,"*
>
>   (James 1: 2-4).

As such, there are times God may actually cause a hardship or suffering to accomplish a greater purpose.

The crucible of life suffering can also accomplish a refining of our character and life mission:

> *"In this you greatly rejoice, even though now for a little while, if necessary, you have been distressed by various trials, that the proof of your faith, being more precious than gold which is perishable, even though tested by fire, may be found to result in praise and glory and honor at the revelation of Jesus Christ;*

And though you have not seen Him, you love Him, and though you do not see Him now, but believe in Him, you greatly rejoice with joy inexpressible and full of glory, Obtaining as the outcome of your faith the salvation of your souls." (1 Peter 1: 6-9).

As such, there are times God may actually cause a hardship or suffering to accomplish a greater purpose. The thought that God might be behind some of our suffering or pain flies in the face of some who believe (and preach) that God intends a primarily trouble-free life for His followers.

> *However, God's desire for His followers goes beyond comfort in life to conformity to His character and will.*

As J.I. Packer reminds us, "This idea of God's (trouble-free) intention is a mistake: God's wisdom is not, and never was pledged to keep a fallen world happy, or to make loneliness comfortable. Not even Christians has He promised a trouble-free life; rather the reverse. (See John 16: 37 when Jesus promises 'tribulation' for His followers). God has other ends in view for life in this world than simply to make it easy for everyone."[19]

God indeed blesses His children (James 1: 17). However, God's desire for His followers goes beyond comfort in life to conformity to His character and will. God also tests His

---

[19] J.I. Packer.91,92.

children (Psalm 11: 15) with trying circumstances and disciplines them through undesirable struggles to accomplish His greater good (Hebrews 12: 5-14).

God's role in suffering and evil is mixed. At times, He can and actually does cause suffering or inflict judgment through circumstantial means. However when He does so, God always has a greater good or higher intention in mind. At times, God is the direct cause behind our troubles and suffering. He has brought on or allowed *"momentary light affliction"* in order to produce our refined character and a godliness that will assure us a home in Heaven and an experience of *"an eternal weight of glory far beyond all comparison."* (2 Corinthians 4: 17).

God is also an indirect cause of much of what happens. Psalm 8 is a beautiful description of God's careful attention to His creatures and the created universe.

> *"O Lord, our Lord, how majestic is your name in all the earth, who hast displayed your splendor above the heavens! When I consider the heavens, the work of your fingers, the moon and the stars, which you have ordained;What is man that you take thought of him? And the son of man that you care for him?* (Psalm 8: 1, 3, 4).

There is also beautiful prose in Job (chapters 38-41) which describes God's ongoing role in sustaining the created order. A good example of God's daily care is found in 38: 12:

> *"Have you ever in your life commanded the morning or caused the dawn to know its*

place?" God is truly the sustainer of all creation: *"In Him all things hold together."* (Colossians 1: 17).

Many things happen in life simply due to the laws and principles God established to sustain His creation. If someone falls and injures themselves or even dies, the answer to "Why did this bad thing happen to such a good person?" It may simply be, Gravity.

If a person is hell-bent on ascribing every responsibility to God, it is assumed they would say "God caused them to fall." At best, it seems there can only be indirect causality, and it seems like a stretch to hold God responsible every time the law of gravity works when we prefer that it did not.

> *It seems like a stretch to hold God responsible every time the law of gravity works when we prefer that it did not.*

Could it be that many bad accidents happen in life when humans are simply at the wrong place at the wrong time and the laws of physics or inertia simply held true? Yes, these laws are established by God to hold creation together, but to blame God for every such accident seems like a misapplication of a sense of responsibility. There need be no greater or nebulous "everything happens for a reason" explanation than this: God did not consciously direct the accident to happen. The accident simply occurred because natural laws were in effect with tragic outcomes. (People or objects collided in a destructive, damaging or injuring way). There need be no "master plan reason" for why the accident took place, and God is no less in charge.

Likewise, it may be pointless to seek answers to "why" a tornado wipes out a town, including a church and several innocent victims other than the laws of weather and weather patterns were in effect.

> *Could it be that many bad accidents happen in life when humans are at the wrong place at the wrong time and the laws of physics or inertia simply happened?*

The laws of nature account for much in life. Tsunamis, hurricanes, droughts, and floods are often explained by nothing more "mystical" than that's how God created the elements of nature and weather to act.

This is not to say that God never intentionally uses the created order to accomplish His direct will. We accept that it is possible that God can cause natural phenomenon to accomplish a supernatural agenda. The Bible has many examples of nature being used as a tool God not only created, but a tool He is free to use to influence people and the course of human history. From the world-wide flood involving Noah (Genesis 6) to swarms of hornets that drove Israel's enemies from their lands (Joshua 24: 12) the elements of nature are at God's disposal.

> *We have no Biblical reason to assume otherwise than much of what happens in life regarding creation just happens because of the laws and functions God has put in place.*

However, because God can use nature for specific ends doesn't make this the unanimous answer. We have no Biblical reason to assume otherwise than much of what happens in life regarding nature just happens because of the laws and functions of nature God has put in place.

A second cause for why things happen including pain and suffering is simply living on this fallen planet. Due to the spiritually fallen state of this world, sin exists. Evil happens along with all the ugly results that go with it.

Sickness and disease were unleashed on all creatures through our sinful fall near the beginning of time. With this perspective, we need not wrestle for "why" in many cases of personal sickness. Many diseases you or a loved one struggle with may simply be a symptom of the creation-wide devastation of sin. Birth defects may be nothing more than evidence that even the human gene-pool has been tainted by the force of sin.

Death too is a result of Adam's sin that has simply been passed down from one generation to the next. As long as we are awaiting the new Heaven and new Earth promised by God, death will befall us all. It is simply an inescapable by-product of living on a fallen planet. We don't need to blame God as the cause every time death or disease occur.

A third answer to why things happen is human choice. Free will is powerful. God created us with free will from the beginning of creation. He gave Adam and Eve choices along with huge responsibility as seen in Genesis 1: 28 (fill the Earth and subdue it). Rarely does God ever over-ride our choices. The Bible teaches that good, wise, and righteous choices tend to produce desirable outcomes. Likewise, bad, foolish, or evil choices tend to have undesirable results (Galatians 6:7; Deuteronomy 30: 15-20). There are exceptions, but outcomes are largely the result of the decision we or someone else make, and the actions we or they take.

> *Sadly, chemistry (nicotine and other carcinogens) and physiology combined in a disadvantageous way, to produce lung cancer. There need be no gut-wrenching, disillusioning cries to God about "Why did my loved one get cancer?"*

For instance, you may have had a salad today at lunch, because you *chose* a salad, ordered one, and a waitress delivered it to you. Your choice and someone else's choices (the chef to prepare it, the waitress to deliver it) are the simple straightforward reason a salad "happened" at lunch. We don't need to identify God as the ultimate "reason" behind your salad.

This book considers more painful, undesirable "why" events. Our internal life battles center around pain, disappointments, and injustice that significantly impact us or our loved ones.

Some big questions may have a simple answer related to choice. "Why did my loved one get lung cancer?" The answer may be no more complex than they were a chain-smoker for 25 years. Such behavior causes lung cancer. In essence, they made a choice with each of the thousands of cigarettes they smoked that gave them lung cancer. Sadly, chemistry (nicotine and other carcinogens) and physiology combined in a disadvantageous way to produce lung cancer. There need be no gut-wrenching disillusioning cries to God about "Why did my loved one get cancer?"

People often knowingly make bad choices. These bad choices can bring unbearable outcomes, and when they do, we should save the question "Why did this happen?" The straightforward answer may simply be, they or you made a decision(s) that caused it.

This is true of much in life. People succeed or fail in work, relationships, finances and physical health largely due to their decisions and actions; or the decisions and actions of someone else.

"Why did I lose my job?" can often be answered by an honest examination of your work-related behaviors (or someone else's). If you were habitually late and failed at responsibilities and consistently missed deadlines, there is little guesswork. You got fired because you didn't make choices to act like a good and worthwhile employee. Perhaps the owner embezzled funds and just got arrested. In this case, the answer isn't about you. You lost your job because of the evil someone else did. Much of "Why bad things happen" is due to the reason that you or someone else chose and acted in a way that caused it, that's why.

> *Much of why bad things happen is due to the reason: "You or someone else chose and acted in a way that caused it, that's why."*

A fourth and final cause for what happens is that Satan directly or indirectly caused it. The late comedian "Flip" Wilson was famous for his comedic claim, "The Devil made me do it!" This isn't quite the point. We all have free will and each of us is responsible for our choices. Just as God rarely over-rides free will, Satan doesn't either. He is limited primarily to influencing our behavior through sinful temptations, or through trying us in difficult ways permitted through divine providence.

If a person chooses to do illegal drugs, commit rape or a violent crime, tell a lie or steal, the choice was theirs and they are responsible. This is a combination of Satan's temptation and their behavioral yielding to sin. Some of Satan's greatest work is in tempting people to make evil, pain-inflicting, destructive choices to themselves or to someone else. Still, the yielding choice is ours (James 1: 14, 15). We are the ultimate reason for the bad choice.

> *Some of Satan's greatest work is in tempting people to make evil, pain-inflicting, destructive choices affecting themselves or someone else.*

The force of sin is destructive and deadly. The Bible tells us in Romans 5: 12 that death entered the human race through the sin Adam committed. Death, disease, suffering, and evil are the direct and indirect results of sin, the spiritual force emanating from Satan. Through his evil, diabolical influence, Satan has wreaked havoc and caused incredible direct and indirect pain on humanity and all of God's creation.

In spite of most of Satan's work being through temptation or in the indirect results of a sin-marred planet, there are times in the Bible when it appears he is directly involved in inflicting human pain and suffering. It would appear from Job 1: 12 and 2: 6 that divine permission must be given in order for Satan to make a direct attack on us. We can only assume from the context of Job 1: 1, 2 that such permission is rare and infrequent. In the Gospels we see Jesus speak of permission Satan sought and received to "sift Peter like wheat" (Luke 22: 37).

Satan's original success was in tempting Adam and Eve to sin. Once they did, it opened the floodgates of Hell upon humanity. Sickness, disease, death, evil and injustice were infused into the human race. Hereditary predispositions to certain diseases, deformities, and addictions indicate that even the human gene-pool has been afflicted by sin.

An understanding of Satan's direct and indirect role in causing pain and suffering alleviates some of our anguished wonderings. For example: The answer to "Why, was my child/grandchild born with this horrible disease or deformity" may simply be that the pervasive impact of sin has physiologically devastated the human race through physical pain, birth defects, disease and suffering since the beginning. Such heartache is simply and tragically a symptom of living in a sin-stained world."

> *Hereditary predispositions to certain diseases, deformities and addictions indicate that even the human gene-pool has been afflicted by sin.*

In this context of understanding, it is unlikely to assume and unnecessary to explain that such heartaches are a direct act of Satan personally targeting your baby.

Much of our pain and heartache is an indirect consequence of Satan's sinful fall and his hateful efforts to involve as much of humanity as possible in evil and the dreaded consequences it brings. The death, evil and disease Satan brought to God's creation strikes us all. This fallen-ness is inescapable and creation-wide; no life can be totally immune.

As the apostle Paul put it: *"For we know that the whole of creation groans and suffers the pains of childbirth together until now"* (Romans 8: 22).

APPLICATION AND REFLECTION:

To review this chapter, the universe is governed in such a way that the Bible speaks of four possible causes for what happens in life:

First, God obviously exercises control in this world. "He changes the times and the seasons…He removes kings and establishes kings…" (Daniel 2: 21). God is an all-powerful God and He is active in His creation

Many things that happen God indirectly causes as a result of the laws and dynamics God has established to sustain His creation.

Second, much of life is a result of the fallen condition of our planet.. As such, a good deal of our suffering is simply a by-product of the destructive nature of sin.

Third, Human choice is responsible for an overwhelming amount of what happens. Good, Godly choices typically yield good results and vice-versa. Still, it is not guaranteed that bad brings bad and good always yields good.

Finally, Satan has a will and a plan to destroy or at least damage all God has created for good. Many victims will find no answer to why some great evil happened to them other than someone yielded to sinful temptation and chose to commit such a sin at their expense.

1. How can the possibility of four causes lessen the emotional load of trying to figure out why bad things happen?
2. Do you agree with this paradigm? Why or why not?

CHAPTER INTRODUCTION

CHAPTER SEVEN: "Now what?" Thirteen suggestions to deal with bad things and "unanswered" prayers.

"I know that you can do all things, and that no purpose of yours can be thwarted...I have declared things which I did not understand, things too wonderful for me, which I did not understand" (Job 42: 2, 3).

> Job came to the same conclusion that all of us should. God is all powerful, all good, all knowing, and we can never truly understand His ways. Many times, the most helpful question to ask in the face of life's hardships is not "why" but **"now what?"**

> You may be going through a rough time now, perhaps you are in one of the darkest seasons of life in your recent memory. Maybe your course in life requires you to cope with an ongoing situation that doesn't seem to change. Your pain may be relational, physical, or situational.

> Each of the following suggestions ends with an italicized possible prayerful response. Use these thoughts to prompt your own prayers in the midst of your struggles.

> Remember, God loves and cares for you. He wants you to trust Him, more than He wants you to figure Him and this world out. Learn to ask "Now what?" more than "Why?"

CHAPTER SEVEN: "Now what?" Thirteen suggestions to deal with bad things and "unanswered" prayers.

1. **Don't ask "why?" ask "now what?"**

The book of Job is a forty two chapter example that God isn't as interested in us understanding "why?" as much as we seem to be. At the end of this painful biography, God answers Job's lament and his friends' self-righteous accusations with a basic "I'm God and you're not. If I don't think you need to know or understand, choose to accept that." The book of Job makes it clear God is far more interested in us learning to trust Him than learning how to figure Him (and life) out!

Job would tell us that one of the most difficult, disillusioning and unanswered questions men and women seem to ask of life's big tragedies is "why" A much better question to ask God is "now what?"

Paul shows how "now what?" can benefit us when there is no answer to "why." According to his writings in Galatians 4: 13-15 and 6: 11 Paul appeared to have had some sort of debilitating eye disease. No doubt Paul sought prayer and healing for this ongoing condition. This eye disease may have been the "thorn in the flesh" Paul speaks of in his letter to the Corinthians. Paul stated that his pleading for healing on three occasions was fruitless.

Paul accepted God's answer of no to healing the eye disease, and opened his heart and mind to consider "Now what." Paul's willingness to let go of his request for healing and learn more about God, added a timeless and encouraging truth to Paul, and to all of us who read his words:

> "Concerning this (thorn in the flesh) I entreated the Lord three times that it might depart from me. And He has said to me, 'My grace is sufficient for you, for power is perfected in weakness,' most gladly, therefore, I will rather boast about my weaknesses, that the power of Christ may dwell in me.
>
> I am well content with weaknesses, with insults, with distresses, with persecutions, with difficulties for Christ's sake, for when I am weak, then I am strong." 2 Corinthians 12: 7-10

There is great growth potential in our times of suffering and struggle. Most admirable

> *There is great growth potential in our times of suffering and struggle. Most admirable character qualities were forged through the refining fires of life's' hardships, not on the beach on vacation.*

character qualities were forged through the refining fires of life's hardships, not on the beach during vacation. There is likewise an intimacy with God available to us in suffering that is not there any other time. Paul calls it "The fellowship of His (Christ's) sufferings."

Look for lessons to be learned in the hardships and pain of life. Pain can get our attention like few things can. C.S. Lewis identifies the value of pain. "If the first and lowest operation of pain shatters the illusion that all is well, the second shatters the illusion that what we have, whether good or bad, in itself is our own and enough for us."[20]

Pain, heartache and injustice can create just enough dissatisfaction with life to put us in search of something more. If we let it, pain opens us to other perspectives and priorities and to a deeper and different pursuit of God and who He is. *In place of constantly asking God to provide more creature comforts, we can pray "God, I accept your amazing grace, I release my agenda, and ask your guidance of my heart and my response to "now what?"*

2. **Don't blame God:**

One of the most outstanding statements about Job during his entire life tragedy is in Job 1: 22.

> *"Through all this Job did not sin, nor did he blame God."*

Job struggled greatly with trying to figure out why everything was happening. The condescending consolations of His self-righteous friends made Job's quest for answers even more difficult. Job debated back at his friends and cried out to God for understanding. God finally responded to Job in

---

[20] Lewis. P. 94.

chapters 38-41. He begins with a summary of His wondrous deeds and excellent greatness. God never gives Job an explanation as to the "Why?" for his pain and suffering. If all this happened for a reason, God gave Job no indication of what that reason was.

It is as if God's conclusive response to Job is simply "I'm God and you're not; I owe no one an explanation." In the end Job realized and accepted the fact that some things in life were never meant to be understood. He did not stay stuck in his quest to answer "Why?"

> *If all this happened for a reason, God gave Job no indication of what that reason was.*

In your suffering, learn to be like Job. Job was able to trust God and not blame him. The less we blame God, the easier it is to trust Him. *Prayerfully, out loud, remind yourself and God with a simple, "God I will not blame you. I trust you, even when I don't understand."*

3. <u>Don't sin in your suffering.</u>

In addition to not blaming God, the Bible observes another amazing thing about Job in 2: 10. *"In all this (suffering) Job did not sin with his lips."* Prolonged pain or devastating loss can bear down on us in such a way that our stress turns into a verbal attack on others. It's easy to take our stress out on others. Job didn't do that, he didn't sin against others with what he said. His language stayed appropriate. He didn't turn his pain into angry, hateful outbursts.

Such sinful outbursts would have been easy and seemed justified. Job's own wife mocked his integrity and trust in God. Still, Job didn't curse his wife or vent his pain sideways at her.

> *God doesn't sweep away our resentful words with an "Oh, they don't really mean it, they're just **upset** right now." Don't sin with your lips, against others or against God.*

Neither did Job sin against God with what he said in the midst of his pain and loss. He could have followed his wife's foolish advice and cursed God in his pain. He could have been like the ancient Israelites and grumbled against God in his hardship. It's important to note that God views our grumbling as rebellion, and lack of trust in Him. (Read Deuteronomy 1: 27, 32; Psalm 106: 25-27).

a

Many people today advise sufferers to feel free with what they say to and about God under the guise "It's ok, God can take it." Use caution with your words when you are in pain. Be honest with God, express yourself passionately in prayer, but trust God in your pain and let your words reflect it. God doesn't sweep away our resentful words with an "Oh, they don't really mean it; they're just upset right now." Don't sin with your lips against others or against God.

If you've been playing the blame game and venting your anger against God or others, take a moment to apologize: *"Dear God, please forgive me. In my limited understanding, like Job's wife, I've been blaming you for what I don't understand. Whatever the cause, whatever the course of my future will be, I trust you with a grateful heart. Likewise, please forgive me for hurting others in my own pain, and give me the grace to not sin against anyone else in my struggles."*

4. **Be humble in hardship.**

One of the most important things pain and hardship can do if you let it, is to move you out of the center of your universe. Humility is one of the three bottom line attributes God values according to Micah 6: 8.

> "He has told you, o man, what is good and what the Lord requires of you but to do justice, to love kindness and to walk humbly with your God."

In His self-description, Jesus tells His disciples two of His most defining qualities are humility and gentleness.

Humility matters to God. In the Old Testament God recognized Moses as the most humble man on the face of the Earth (Numbers 12: 3). In the New Testament in

His self-description, Jesus tells His disciples two of His most defining qualities are humility and gentleness (Matthew 11: 29).

In the Bible, when people had a genuine revelation of God, it was a sobering realization of the absolute holiness and magnificence of God. Moses hid his face in fear when he encountered God at the burning bush (Exodus 3: 6). Isaiah cried out *"Woe is me for I am ruined. My eyes have seen the King, the Lord of hosts"* (Isaiah 6: 4). Even Peter, James and John, Jesus' closest disciples, fell on their faces in fear as they encountered Christ on the mount of transfiguration (Matthew 17: 6). The proper human response toward an Awesome God, in any setting in life, is humility, reverence, and a loving trusting submission. Humility allows us to accept life with grace.

Inversely, when I'm the center of my universe I demand my way, my wants and my comforts. When the world revolves around me and life is not going the way I planned; I demand answers, and I want an explanation. I complain, feel sorry for myself, or get bitter.

Job displayed humility in hardship. He didn't feel like he was too good to suffer. Job didn't act like God owed him better than what he was receiving. This is clearly seen right after Job lost his children, his wealth and his health. Job's wife was bitter at the "undeserved" calamity and advised Job to "Curse God and die." Job met her angry arrogance with humble acceptance of hardship in Job 2: 10:

"You speak as one of the foolish (center-of-their-universe) women speaks. Shall we indeed accept good from God and not accept adversity?"

Job was in no way fond of his hardships, but he did not display the angry arrogance that demanded answers. Job was humble enough to accept adversity, humble enough to seek God, and humble enough to trust God in his pain. Learn to do the same. Ask God, *Please use my struggle to open the eyes of my heart to any arrogance or lack of humility. Teach me to be like Christ, and use this circumstance to fashion the Fruit of the Spirit in my character: Love, Joy, Peace, Patience, Kindness, Goodness, Faithfulness, Gentleness, Self-Control"* (Galatians 5: 22, 23).

> *Indulging ourselves in personal sympathy must seem petty to our God who is working out a creation-wide plan of redemption. Stop being surprised by pain.*

5. Learn to expect good and bad in life.

When we realize the universe is at war (God versus Satan or eternal life versus sin) and that we are no longer the center of the universe, it puts life into perspective. We live on a fallen planet, and we are fallen from God's original intentions.

Many of our prayers focus on us asking God to change the consequences of living on a fallen planet...now! This world is such a mess that even God can't "fix" it as it is. Jesus tells a parable about an enemy sowing weeds in a landowner's field. Servants want to pull out all the weeds, but the wise farmer knows trying to pull out all the weeds will also destroy the rest of the field. Jesus told this story as an analogy for our fallen world. (Matthew 13: 24-30). God won't "pull" all the evil from creation. The best He can do is provide a path of salvation from this fallen planet (weed-infested field) so that someday we can spend eternity with God in a divine pain and evil free new heaven and a new Earth (Revelation 21: 1).

At the same time, the Bible encourages us to take pain and suffering in stride.

When we accept that we live on a sin-corrupted planet, pain, hardship, and evil should come as no surprise. Questions like "Why is this pain happening to me?" seem small and self-focused. Indulging ourselves in personal sympathy must seem petty to our God who is working out a creation-wide plan of redemption. Do yourself a favor, stop being surprised by pain. Stop telling yourself "This shouldn't be happening." Stop getting overwhelmed because "You don't deserve this."

Much of the negativity in our lives is simply a direct or indirect consequence of "the fall." Therefore, learn to accept good and bad. Rejoice over every pleasant and desired blessing you receive. Give thanks with a grateful heart daily. Celebrate goodness and good things.

At the same time, the Bible encourages us to take pain and suffering in stride. James instructs us to *"Consider it all joy when you encounter various trials!"* (James 1: 2). Jesus told His followers in Matthew 5: 45, *"God causes his sun to rise on the evil and the good, He sends rain on the righteous and the unrighteous."* Jesus was well aware of the impact sin has had on creation. Sin and the fall of humanity are the reason Christ came *"to seek and save the lost."* (Luke 19: 10).

> Christ gives us a good reality check in the Sermon on the Mount. His remarks provide a healthy view of the world we live in:
>
> *"Therefore, do not be anxious for tomorrow; for tomorrow will care for itself. Each day has enough trouble of its own."* (Matthew 6: 34).

Stop acting like God owes you or promised you a trouble free life. Jesus himself lived in this troubled world and promised us both blessings and hardships. Blessings and hardships go hand in hand and God can and should be trusted and thanked in every circumstance. Learn to be grateful in the best, and in the worst of circumstances. The Apostle Paul's advice in 1 Thessalonians 5: 16-18 applies in desired and undesired situations alike:

> *"Rejoice always pray without ceasing. In everything give thanks, for this is God's will for you in Christ Jesus."*

Pray often the famous Serenity Prayer attributed to the late theologian Reinhold Neibuhr which applies in the good and bad in life:

> *"God grant me the grace to accept with serenity the things I cannot change, courage to change the things which should be changed, and the wisdom to distinguish one from the other.*
>
> *Living one day at a time, enjoying one moment at a time, accepting hardship as a pathway to peace, taking as Jesus did, this sinful world as it is, not as I would have it, trusting that you will make all things right, if I surrender to Your will so that I shall be reasonably happy in this life and supremely happy with You forever in the next. Amen."*[21]

6. Remember four possible causes for everything.

The why of circumstances often alludes us. Remember four potential causes. This four-fold causality will invite broader conclusions than the two extremes "God is to blame or Satan is attacking me."

---

[21] Reinhold Neihbuhr. From a sermon at Heath Evangelical Union Church in Heath, Massachusettes. Phillipp and Carol Zaeliski, Prayer: A History. Houghton Mifflin: 2005. P. 127.

A. As a direct **act of God** in accordance with His providential will.

B. Life is often just a function of the created (and fallen) world we live in. As a result of living on a **fallen planet,** we get sick or because the natural laws of the **created order** are in effect. For example, I let go of a plate and gravity brought it crashing to the ground.

C. Many things happen because of **human will.** I or someone else made a choice and it had consequences either good or bad.

D. Finally, some things happen as an attack of **Satan**.

Having this four-fold understanding of causality sheds clarifying light on the implications of the claim "Everything happens for a reason." With this fourfold perspective, we can be in hearty agreement, YES, this happened for a reason. This four-fold perspective simply broadens the potential reasons for why something might have happened, and to de-mystify life a bit.

> *You will live in much greater peace if you can live without always having to know "Why?"*

It is sometimes helpful to search for answers to why things happen in our lives. Learning and growth can occur. However, as we consider the good and bad in life, hopefully we will have the humility and grace to accept that we will not understand many things that happen. Even if we never understand, God doesn't really owe us an explanation. You will live in much greater peace if you can live without always having to know "why?"

An appropriate prayer is simply, *"God, when you don't answer my desperate pleas with an awesome miracle, help me to rest contently in your amazing grace"* (2 Corinthians 12: 9).

7. Observe the law of sowing and reaping.

A good amount of answers to the question "Why did this bad or good thing happen?" could be answered by the simple concept of causality. Scientists call it cause and effect. The laws of physics explain "For every action there is an equal and opposite reaction." Simply put, actions cause things to happen.

The Bible speaks in terms of sowing and reaping. The concept is simple and ubiquitous throughout creation. If you sow (plant) a cucumber seed, you reap (harvest) cucumbers not tomatoes. Results to most actions are not a total surprise.

If you push on the accelerator the vehicle will move, push harder and it will move faster, push hard enough and the vehicle will be difficult to control. Fill out several job applications and you will likely get a response, possibly an interview, and eventually a job. Fill out no applications and you can expect no interviews, and likewise no job.

Sowing and reaping, cause and effect are so readily observable from infancy through adulthood that we accept them and nearly take them for granted. Flip on a light switch, the light goes on; turn on a faucet, the water comes out; hit someone in anger, get in trouble…or a fight! Cause and effect, sowing and reaping surround us. We accept this principle, EXCEPT when we don't want it to work.

I may complain and perhaps even blame God about my loved one having a heart attack. I may ask "why God?" or get angry that it doesn't seem fair." All the while, I ignore the cause of the heart attack. My loved one had horrible eating habits, was significantly overweight, had unaddressed high blood pressure and cholesterol, and never exercised. In this scenario, it is simply unfair and irrational to blame God. Responsibility rests primarily with my loved one and perhaps some heredity.

> *Ask yourself "Did I or someone cause this?" If the answer is yes, turn the pain or difficulty into a learning experience not a blame-game!*

So, how many bad things happen as a by-product of the law of sowing and reaping? Ask yourself "Did I or someone, through a decision or behavior, cause this?" If the answer is yes, turn the pain or difficulty into a learning experience, not a blame-game!

Our struggle comes when bad things happen in spite of good character or good decisions and efforts: when a good employee unfairly loses their job; when a person who works at being reasonably healthy dies of a heart attack, and so on. In such cases the law of sowing and reaping isn't in effect and our struggle for "why" can be difficult. Bad things happened that weren't deserved. When actions bring

> *However, sin causes complication, pain, regret, shame and dysfunction...eventually.*

consequences, our prayer can actually be *"I thank you Lord, that you are a just God. As a result, we tend to reap what we sow. Give me grace to grow, learn and accept this current reality in my life and work it toward some good for your glory."*

8. <u>Deal with sin.</u>

In chapters 29-33 of Deuteronomy, Moses clarified a spiritual principle: the eventual consequences of sin are devastating while the eventual consequences of righteousness are delightful. Moses called the people to personal responsibility in their life choices:

> *"I have set before you life and death, the blessing and the curse. So choose life in order that you may live, you and your descendants"* (Deuteronomy 30: 19b).

Initially, sinful choices are enjoyable or beneficial. That's why sinful temptations are so tempting! Think about sexual pleasure, the "good feeling" from alcohol or drug use, the trouble you avoid with a lie, or "juicy" gossip-laden conversations. The list goes on. While pleasing at first, sin causes complication, pain, regret, shame and dysfunction...eventually. The Bible identifies the temporary pleasures of sin in Hebrews 11: 25.

> *The reason God says "Don't sin" is to spare us from the complication, pain, regret, shame and dysfunction that sin eventually brings.*

> *"Moses chose rather to endure ill-treatment with the people of God, than to enjoy the passing pleasures of sin."*

People unfamiliar with the Bible can mistakenly refer to it as "a book of do's and don'ts." They accuse the Bible of being interested in killing their joy and fun. This is a misperception. The reason God says "Don't sin" is to spare us from the complication, pain, regret, shame and the dysfunction that sin eventually brings. Think of all the STD's, divorce, relational pain, jail time, and abuse that would not exist if people simply avoided sin and obeyed God's word.

Sin brings consequences. It is important to note that God can forgive us of any sin, but rarely does He undo the law of sowing and reaping by removing the practical consequences for our wrong. For example: God will forgive you of your DWI offense, but you may still lose your license, do jail time, or pay a fine.

Let the pain from your sin or someone else's sin move you to seek or give forgiveness. First, seek forgiveness from God by asking in prayer. Second, forgive yourself for what you have repented of. Third, when applicable, seek forgiveness from the person you have sinned against. Likewise, let the painful outcomes of your sin discipline you to make Godly choices and have healthier relational boundaries.

There are also times that the sin we must deal with is not our own. A common answer to "why" something bad happens is because much of the evil and pain we experience can be due to someone's sin against us: their lies, their violence, their unfaithfulness, etc. Learning to forgive is the best practice for victims.

When we are sinned against, we must guard against un-forgiveness. Harboring un-forgiveness will yield what the Bible calls a root of bitterness, and we the victim end up "paying" even more for sins committed against us:

> *"See to it that no one comes short of the grace of God; that no root of bitterness*

springing up causes trouble, and by it many be defiled." (Hebrews 12: 15)

Forgiveness does not mean acting like the offense didn't happen or enabling further bad behavior. Forgiveness is simply choosing to no longer hold the person's offense against them.

Forgiveness does not remove the need for justice to be served. Justice for wrongdoing is often essential to bring evildoers to repentance.

Likewise, forgiving someone doesn't mean we continue to let them hurt us. Forgiveness often requires establishing healthy relational boundaries that are necessary to protect oneself from someone else's sinful choices.

A final consideration is in dealing with "sin in the family tree." The Bible talks about sin passing from one generation to the next (Exodus 20: 5). We learn righteous and unrighteous habits from our families. You may be the victim of sin from your parents, grandparents or some other relative. These include alcoholism, anger issues, unfaithfulness or abuse, to name a few.

With God's grace, you can heal from their damage and learn not to repeat the sin you "inherited." Be encouraged! You don't need to repeat the sins of your family. You can change what you pass down to generations after you. Read the story of Joseph for a good example of this in Genesis 37-50.

Ask God to help you forgive the offender and heal from what they did to you. Ask Him to help you resist the temptation to carry on so you don't repeat their sin, or sin in some other way in retaliation against what was done.

"Lord, I thank you that the Bible assures me that you forgive my sins whenever I ask (1 John 1: 9). Help me always to seek and walk in forgiveness as often as necessary, and to grant it to others as often as needed. Help me learn from sin and leave it, rather than habitually repeat it in my life."

9. Pass the test.

The Bible repeatedly refers to the fact that God tests us. God uses challenging life experiences and decisions to test the condition of our hearts (Jeremiah 11: 20, 20: 12; Psalm 11: 5; Proverbs 17: 3; 1 Thessalonians 2: 4). Hebrews 11: 7 mentions how even Abraham, a man who was called the "friend of God" had his heart tested in obedience:

> *The book of Job makes it clear God is far more interested in us learning to trust Him, than learning how to figure Him and life out!*

"By faith Abraham, when he was tested, offered up Isaac..."

If God tests the righteous, even someone like Abraham, He will test you. God doesn't just test us in tough decisions of obedience; God tests us regarding whether or not we trust Him in difficult and painful experiences. Trials and suffering are testing times meant to refine us:

> *"In this you greatly rejoice, even though now for a little while; if necessary, you have been distracted by various trials, that the proof of your faith, being more precious than gold, which is perishable, even though tested by fire, may be found to result in praise and honor at the revelation of Jesus Christ"* (1 Peter 1: 6, 7).

God intends to test you with some of the hardship, pain and suffering in life. It should not be a mystery that some of our prayers for deliverance are unanswered if we are asking God to spare us from a "test" He wants us to experience. He is testing your trust and dependence on Him. God tests your love for Him versus your love for this world.

Remember to meet each test with an attitude of gratitude. Some of our most powerful responses in times of testing are outward expressions of gratitude for God's blessings, in spite of our struggles. Be confident you WILL pass the test, and grow and please God in the process!

When facing adversity, rather than prayers obsessed with "God get me out of this!" It may be more appropriate to ask *"Lord, is this a test? How are you wanting me to grow through this? How can this struggle be used to refine me? In spite of my current difficulties, I thank you for the many blessings in my life. Grant me the wisdom, self-control and strength to grow, to give you glory, and to pass this test."*

10. Turn the test into a testimony.

God will never waste the pain and suffering in our lives. If we let Him, He will somehow use it for good. The Apostle Paul experienced a great deal of hardship in his life. In addition to physical illness, he was unjustly treated and abused. He was stoned, imprisoned, shipwrecked, often lacked food or shelter, the list is extensive. (Read 2 Corinthians 11: 23-27). Still, the following verse shows how an abiding optimism is seen in Paul's life and letters.

> *God will never waste the pain and suffering in our lives. If we let Him, He will somehow use it for good.*

"And we know that God causes all things to work together for good to those who love God, to those who are called according to His purpose." (Romans 8: 28)

Romans 8: 28 doesn't mean the problem goes away, the unfairness is undone or the disease is healed, or the initial prayer is eventually granted after all. Paul is simply reminding us that God will use our struggles to teach us, to equip us, and to grow us. However, this verse is somewhat dependent on our cooperation. We must not turn a deaf ear or hardened heart toward what God wants to do in our circumstances.

The Bible is full of many who benefited from pain. Sarah endured embarrassing infertility, David overcame army-wide fear and faced a hateful warrior-giant, Daniel was deported as a political prisoner from his homeland. Yet, for each of these, the truth of Romans 8: 28 eventually happened and God worked some good from the situation.

When we stay humble, trust God, and maintain the patient heart of a learner, God can turn your test into a testimony. It may be a testimony of learning to persevere in prayer until an answer comes. It may be a testimony of God re-directing you or using your failure to accomplish some greater good. It may be a testimony of how God grew you personally through struggle or has become more real to you through your pain.

Look back on your life at how often a test turned out for good. Share that as a testimony with others regarding God's faithfulness in your life. At the same time, let that realization build confidence in you for the testimonies in process, with God's help you will prevail!

Trust God. He can turn the test into a testimony through you. *"Dear God, I trust that you will take this current struggle and somehow bring about some good. I trust you and choose to depend on your love and grace, I will not become blameful or bitter. This test will become a testimony of your work and your goodness in my life. Amen"*

11. <u>Grow closer to God in and because of your pain.</u>

In *The Problem of Pain* C.S. Lewis states: "Pain insists on being attended to. God whispers to us in our pleasures, speaks in our conscience, but shouts in our pain. It is His megaphone to rouse a deaf world."[22] Pain gets our attention. It often lingers longer than we ever imagined it would.

Understandably we prefer blessings instead of pain. Blessings are meant to bring gratitude and joy (Psalm 103: 5). They are benevolently bestowed by a loving God. Unfortunately, unlike lingering pain, over time, blessings can get taken for granted. Our gratitude fades, and eventually blessings become an expectation.

Pain is different. Pain often remains, anguish, heartache, injustice and disappointment can all occupy a lingering place in our souls.

> *Because of the "staying power" of our hard times, suffering and our yearning for relief can be a powerful influence for intimacy with God.*

Because of the "staying power" of our hard times, suffering and our yearning for relief can be a powerful influence for intimacy with God. 2 Corinthians 2: 3-5 speaks of the abundance of suffering in this life, along with the abundant response of Christ to such hurts:

> *"Blessed be the God and father of our Lord Jesus Christ, the father of mercies and God of all comfort; who comforts us in all our affliction so that we may be able to comfort those who are in any affliction with the comfort with which we ourselves have been comforted by God.*

---

[22] C.S. Lewis. p.91.

For just as the sufferings of Christ are ours in abundance so also our comfort is abundant through Christ."

In our pain, we have a choice. Do we shake a clenched fist at God in blame and anger, or do we extend an outstretched hand, reaching for a comforting embrace? The Psalmist talks about the trust and safety he felt going through the "valley of the shadow of death" in Psalm 23: 4.

The late Andrae Crouch sang "If I never had a problem, I'd never know that God could solve them. I'd never know what faith in His word could do. Through it all, I've learned to trust I Jesus...and to depend upon His word."[23] Turn your trials into intimate dependence upon and trust in God. Learn to receive comfort and wisdom rather than vent bitterness and anger. God longs to use our struggles to build trust and closeness, not disillusionment.

> *Many Christians get disillusioned with God and frustrated in faith when life doesn't go as they longed or prayed for.*

"Lord, as the Apostle Paul found intimacy with you in 'the fellowship of His sufferings,' help me to be mindful that you were also called 'a man of sorrows and acquainted with grief' (Isaiah 53: 7) Draw me near to you

---

[23] Andrae Crouch. "Through it all" 1973. Sony/ATV Music Publishing LLC. Kobalt Music Publishing Lts., Universal Music Publishing Group.

in and through my pain and struggles, that I might know you more."

12. <u>Learn that "shall" is not "is."</u>

If there is one thing struggles can do if we let them, they can teach us to love this world a little less. It is true, God created this universe. In all its fullness there is great pleasure to be had in this life. There is beauty to be enjoyed, and love to be found in this world. The Bible affirms that there is much to be celebrated and thankful for in life.

However, this world is not our forever home. As Jesus put it, His followers are "in yet not of this world" (John 17: 14-19). Popular Christian songs do good to remind us "we are not home yet." Jesus came to declare and build the Kingdom of Heaven; in men's hearts and in the forever future. Many Christians get disillusioned with God and frustrated in faith when life doesn't go as they longed or prayed for. Many try to apply their faith to minimize pain and suffering and maximize comfort and blessings. They rebuke negatives and claim positives in Jesus' name.

In such attempts, Christians still fail to bring paradise to present day. They will always fail in that regard because Heaven isn't here yet! In Revelation we are told that God is preparing an evil-free and pain-free new Heaven and new Earth. In this paradise-restored we are told God **shall** wipe away every tear, and there **shall** no longer be any death, mourning or crying (Revelation 21: 1-5). This is a future yet to come. Death, mourning, crying, tears are part of our present world. This world is fallen and polluted by sin; the next world is perfect and pain-free. In that new Heaven and Earth, there shall be no more pain, crying or death. The Apostle Paul reminded us that Heaven is so great it surpasses our greatest imagination:

> *"What no eye has seen, what no ear has heard, and what no human mind has conceived, the things God has prepared for those who love Him."* (1 Corinthians 2: 9)

There is or should be an appropriate, subtle homesickness that lingers in the heart of every Christ-follower, for our heavenly home. The joys and pleasures of this world should remind us that incomparable joy awaits us. Likewise Paul reminds us that heartaches and pain ought to point us to what lies ahead:

> *"For I consider the sufferings of this present life are not worthy to be compared to the glory that is to be revealed to us."* (Romans 8: 18)

> *There is (or should be) an appropriate, subtle "homesickness" that lingers in the heart of every Christ-follower, for our heavenly home.*

Rather than discouraging you in your faith, let each of life's struggles put a longing in you for your eternal home. When the pain and injustice seem overwhelming, let it remind you there shall someday be a pain-free, totally just and perfect kingdom in which you will forever live.

When you are disappointed in yourself or someone else, when your dreams seem only that, let it turn your anticipation to another time and another place. Look forward to Jesus, in Heaven, the place He is preparing for you:

> *"And though you have not seen Him, you love Him, and though you do not see Him now, but believe in Him, you greatly rejoice with joy inexpressible and full of glory, obtaining as the outcome the salvation of your souls."* 1 Peter 1: 8.9.

May our prayer be *"Lord, my current struggles make me grateful that you love me enough to prepare a place for me in Heaven. There I will be with you in the absence of pain and evil forever. Even so, Lord Jesus, come quickly!"*

13. Don't go it alone.

Pain and suffering can be isolating. Illness and accidents can separate us from our daily routine and interactions. Grief and loss can negatively impact former relationships; for instance, once a spouse dies "couple friendships" can seem strained. Divorce often damages other relationships beyond the immediately impacted husband and wife. The list goes on and on.

In addition to the kinds of isolation just mentioned, pain and suffering can also cause us to want to withdraw socially. It is not uncommon for people who are suffering to say that they just want to be alone.

Unfortunately, isolation doesn't mix well with pain and suffering, at least not for the person who is struggling. The negative impact of the emotional and even the physical load of pain and suffering is usually lessened when it is shared with trusted people who care.

The Bible admonishes us to help others deal with their pain. *"Bear one another's burdens and thereby fulfill the law of Christ."* (Galatians 6: 2). Romans 12: 15 makes it clear that highly emotional experiences should be shared: *"Rejoice with those who rejoice, and weep with those who weep."* When joy is shared, it gets magnified, when sorrow or pain get shared, it gets minimized.

> *Resist the temptation to withdraw from family, friends and acquaintances.*

You may be going through a difficult season as you have read this book. Resist the temptation to withdraw from family, friends and acquaintances. This isn't to suggest that you have to bear your soul to everyone you meet and constantly tell them all about your deep dark pain. Relational involvement is healthy for us regardless of what is going on in life.

You may need to force yourself to engage with people, do it anyway. In at least a few relationships, share some of your struggle. It is amazing how problems that seem overwhelming in our minds lessen as we talk about them with a friend who cares. They may not be able to solve your situation or make it go away; but talking about struggles and just being heard is healthy for you and is often a first step toward better coping, and toward discovering possible solutions.

Finally, tell your troubles to God. Job obviously told God repeatedly about his pain and the questions and accusations he battled. When you pray about your problems, it is often helpful to do so out loud. King David modeled this.

> *"In my distress I called upon the Lord, and cried to my God for help; He heard my voice out of his temple, and my cry for help before Him came into His ears"* (Psalm 18: 6)

The remainder of the Psalm celebrates God hearing and responding to David's cries.

Even when our cries for help aren't yet answered, it is good to tell God about your struggles. The Apostle Paul identifies the Holy Spirit as our comforter. Surely in times of pain, heartache or stress, comfort that reaches soul-deep is what we need.

> *Even when our cries for help aren't yet answered, it is good to tell God about your struggles.*

> *"Blessed be the God and Father of our Lord Jesus Christ, the Father of mercies and God of all comfort, who comforts us in all our affliction so that we will be able to comfort those who are in any affliction with the comfort with which we ourselves are*

comforted by God. For just as the sufferings of Christ are ours in abundance, so also our comfort is abundant through Christ" (2 Corinthians 2: 3-5).

Cry out to God in your pain, He is eager to comfort us in our struggles. He also wants to equip us to do the same. As this verse states, once we have suffered and experienced the comfort God and others can bring, we are more able to offer the kind of comfort and support we have received to others who are hurting.

Seek the support, compassion and help of others in times of need. Turn to God as well. As God and others come along-side you in your pain and struggles, learn to do the same in the future with others in your life who need the same.

A helpful prayer might be *"Lord, I am thankful you see me in my situation. I pray for the comfort of the Holy Spirit to help me, and once comforted, help me share the same with others."*

Made in the USA
Lexington, KY
11 October 2017